THE BELIEFNET GUIDE TO

$\mathcal{E}$VANGELICAL $\mathcal{C}$HRISTIANITY

THE BELIEFNET GUIDE TO

Evangelical Christianity

Wendy Murray Zoba

Introduction by
Philip Yancey

Three Leaves Press

Doubleday / New York

THREE
LEAVES
PRESS

PUBLISHED BY DOUBLEDAY
a division of Random House, Inc.

DOUBLEDAY is a registered trademark and THREE LEAVES
PRESS and colophon are trademarks of Random House, Inc.

Library of Congress Cataloging-in-Publication Data

Zoba, Wendy Murray.
   The Beliefnet guide to evangelical Christianity / Wendy
Murray Zoba ; introduction by Philip Yancey.— 1st Three
Leaves Press ed.
      p. cm.—(The Beliefnet guides ; 2)
   Includes bibliographical references (p.).
   (alk. paper)
   1. Evangelicalism. 2. Evangelicalism—History. I. Title.
II. Series.

BR1640.Z63 2005
270.8'2—dc22
2004062068

ISBN 0-385-51452-2

PRINTED IN THE UNITED STATES OF AMERICA

June 2005

First Three Leaves Press Edition

10 9 8 7 6 5 4 3 2 1

CONTENTS

130440

INTRODUCTION BY
PHILIP YANCEY

A friend of mine who runs an inner-city shelter for drug addicts and homeless people and is tantalizingly hard to place on any theological map made this observation: "I love evangelicals. You can get them to do anything. The challenge is, you've also got to soften their judgmental attitudes before they can be effective." As a journalist working primarily within the evangelical milieu, I have seen the truth of his remarks.

Indeed, you can get evangelicals to do anything. This year alone I have seen a variety of evangelicals at work on several continents. In South Africa I spent time with Ray McCauley, a larger-than-life character who in younger days finished second-runner-up to Arnold Schwarzenegger in the Mr. Universe contest. Ray founded a church in Johannesburg based on the charismatic "name it and claim it" philosophy, a church that ultimately grew into the largest in South Africa, with thirty-five thousand members. As the apartheid government began to crumble, Nelson Mandela and Bishop Desmond Tutu embraced Ray, no doubt coveting his nationwide television constituency. In the process Ray's attitudes, politics, and rigid theology began to soften. White members grew disgruntled, and gradually the church's makeup changed in a way that reflects the racial spectrum of the nation: 70 percent black, 10 percent mixed race or "coloured," 10 percent Indian, and 10 percent white. Today Rhema Ministries' many programs include an AIDS hospital and a rehabilitation farm for addicts.

At the other end of the country, in Cape Town, I met Joanna Flanders-Thomas, a dynamic and attractive woman of mixed race. As a student she agitated against the apartheid government. After that nationwide victory she turned to a local problem, the most violent prison in South Africa, where Nelson Mandela had spent several years of confinement. Alone, Joanna started visiting prisoners daily, bringing them a simple Gospel message of forgiveness and reconciliation. She earned their trust, got them to talk about their abusive childhoods, and pointed them to a better way of solving conflicts. The year before her visits began, the prison recorded 279 acts of violence; the next year there were two. Joanna's results attracted the attention of the BBC, which sent a camera crew from London to produce two one-hour documentaries on her work.

Two months later I traveled to Nepal, the world's only Hindu kingdom, a dirt-poor country where the caste system lives on. There I met with leprosy health workers from fifteen nations, mostly European, who serve under an evangelical mission specializing in leprosy work. Historically, most of the major advances in leprosy treatment have come from Christian missionaries—mainly because, as my friend put it, "You can get them to do anything." I met well-trained surgeons, nurses, and physical therapists who devote their lives to caring for leprosy victims, many of them of the Untouchable caste. At their annual conference, the missionaries assembled a makeshift orchestra, sang hymns and prayed together, and shared practical hints on how to handle the Maoist guerrilla threat in Nepal. In their leisure time, some of these missionaries climb the high mountains in Nepal, others focus on bird life, and at least one French doctor studies Himalayan moths. Several had run the Kathmandu marathon, and two had taken a wild motorcycle trek across mountains and rivers into neighboring Tibet. None that I met fit the stereotype of "uptight, right-wing evangelicals," yet all would claim the word *evangelical*. They had come to Nepal, after all, to spread the "good news" implicit in the etymology.

From Nepal I went to Beijing, China, where I attended an international church, two thousand strong, comprising members from sixty nations. An African dance troupe led the music that morning, and the rented hotel room rocked. I met diplomats, business executives, an Oxford philosophy professor, and platoons of young evangelicals who had moved to China in order to teach English and in the process communicate their faith to the Chinese. Government restrictions forbade Chinese nationals from attending the church—ushers checked passports at the door—but later that day I met representatives from the Chinese underground church. In the last thirty years, despite periodic government crackdowns that have led to harsh prison sentences for its leaders, the house church movement has burgeoned into perhaps the largest Christian awakening in history. Experts estimate that 70 million Chinese now worship in house churches scattered throughout the officially atheistic nation. One of the leaders met with me even though authorities had explicitly forbidden it. "I'm eighty-nine years old and I've already spent twenty-three years in prison," he said defiantly. "What are they going to do to me?"

A few months later, in Wisconsin, I attended a conference on ministry to women in prostitution that attracted representatives from thirty different nations. Several dozen evangelical organizations work to counter illegal sex trafficking and also to liberate women from prostitution, which in poor nations constitutes a modern form of slavery. The representatives brought along some of their "clients," who told wrenching tales of abuse and then credited the ministries with setting them free and helping them find new trades.

When I return from such trips and read profiles in *Time* and *Newsweek* about American evangelicals, I feel sad. In the United States, everything eventually boils down to politics, and usually that means polarization. Many Americans view evangelicals as a monolithic voting bloc obsessed with a few moral issues. They miss the vibrancy and enthusiasm, the *good-news-ness* that the word represents in much of the world. Evangelicals in Africa bring food to prisoners, care for AIDS orphans, and operate mission schools that train many of that continent's leaders. There, and in Asia and Latin America, evangelicals also manage microenterprise loan programs that allow families to buy a sewing machine or a flock of chickens. In the last fifty years, the percentage of American missionaries sponsored by evangelical agencies has risen from 40 percent to 90 percent. Presently, about a third of the two billion Christians in the world fall into a category to which the word *evangelical* applies, a large majority of them living outside North America and Europe.

A friend of mine visiting a barrio in São Paulo, Brazil, began to feel anxious as he noticed the minions of drug lords patrolling the neighborhood with automatic weapons. The streets narrowed to dirt paths; plastic water pipes dangled overhead;

and a snarl of wires tapped power from high-voltage lines. The stench of sewage was everywhere. Anxiety increased as he noticed that people inside the tin shacks were glowering at him, a suspicious gringo invading their turf. Was he a narc? An undercover cop? Then the chief drug lord of that neighborhood noticed on the back of his T-shirt the logo of a local Pentecostal church. He broke out in a big smile, "O, *evangelicos!*" he called out, and the scowls turned to smiles. Over the years, that church had extended practical help to the barrio, and now the foreign visitors were joyfully welcomed.

In the United States, too, evangelicals are thriving even as mainline Protestant churches decline. Evangelicals staff many of the five hundred Christian agencies that have sprung up since World War II to combat social problems. Megachurches based on the 17,000-member Willow Creek Community Church near Chicago and Saddleback Community Church in southern California are replicating in major cities. A new, hard-to-classify "emergent church" has evolved to minister to the postmodern generation. In fact, one recent survey revealed that ninety-three of the top one hundred rapidly growing churches in the U.S. identify themselves with evangelicals.

––––––

Truly, you can get evangelicals to do anything. The challenge, as my friend emphasized, is that "you've also got to soften their judgmental attitudes before they can be effective."

When I was writing the book *What's So Amazing About Grace?* I conducted an informal survey among airline seatmates and other strangers willing to strike up a conversation. "When I say the word *evangelical,* what comes to mind?" I would ask.

Often in response I would hear the word *against:* Evangelicals are against abortion, against pornography, against gay rights. Or, I would hear a name like Pat Robertson or Jerry Falwell, two of the most visible, and political, representatives of evangelicalism. For many people I talked to, evangelicals were a force to fear, a gang of moralists attempting to impose their will on a pluralistic society.

A journalist working in the New York media told me that editors had no qualms about assigning a Jewish person to a Jewish story, a Buddhist to a Buddhist story, or a Catholic to a Catholic story, but would never assign an evangelical to an evangelical story. Why not? "They're the ones with an agenda." Evangelicals, according to the New York stereotype, will propagandize and proselytize. You can't trust them. They're judgmental. They have an agenda.

Pollster George Barna found that while 22 percent of Americans say they have a favorable impression of evangelicals, 23 percent report an unfavorable impression. Much of the reason traces back to the perception of evangelicals as a political force, a perception based on a most checkered history.

Until the 1960s, evangelicals were as likely to be aligned with the Democratic Party as the Republican. For example, early in the twentieth century the prominent evangelical William Jennings Bryan, a Democrat, ran unsuccessfully for president and served in Woodrow Wilson's cabinet until he became alarmed over the U.S. tilt toward entering World War I. Evangelicals led the fight for women's suffrage and the abolition of slavery—and also the opposition to it. (Revivalist George Whitefield in the eighteenth century actively campaigned for slavery, and the Southern Baptist denomination later formed over the right of missionaries to own slaves.) At times evangelicals opposed immigration in an attempt to dam the flood of European Catholics.

In perhaps the high-water mark of evangelicals' involvement in politics, they fought successfully for a constitutional amendment decreeing the prohibition of alcohol, a measure later overturned and now viewed with considerable misgiving. Evangelical African-Americans led the civil rights crusade, while some white evangelicals opposed it. In the 1980s, Jerry Falwell urged American Christians to buy gold Krugerrands and to promote U.S. reinvestment in South Africa in an effort to shore up the white regime. Currently, evangelicals take a prominent role in championing the death penalty, supporting pro-life legislation, and retaining traditional definitions of marriage. In short, evangelicals have taken political stances that are sometimes quixotic, sometimes heroic, and often contradictory.

Modern evangelicals in the U.S. increasingly ally themselves with conservative politics. Evangelicals rallied around Ronald Reagan, the nation's first divorced president, who rarely attended church and gave little to charity, while viewing with suspicion Jimmy Carter, a devoutly religious president who taught a Baptist Sunday school class throughout his term in office. Televangelist and preacher Pat Robertson ran for president. So did Gary Bauer, head of the evangelically based Family Research Council. Ralph Reed of the Christian Coalition, who made the cover of *Time* in 1995, served in 2004 as a regional chairman of the Bush-Cheney campaign. To complicate matters, many evangelicals in places like the United Kingdom and New Zealand align themselves with liberal political parties, believing their Christian commitment enjoins them to seek government help for the poor and to oppose war. And in China, many in the underground church see no contradiction in their support for the world's largest Communist government.

———

According to author Randall VanderMey, "Evangelicals tend to view the church not as a giant ship so much as a fleet of rowboats and boogie boards, with each individual in search of an authentic personal experience with God." As we have seen, politics hardly offers the appropriate labels to slap on evangelicals. What descriptors might apply, then? In this book you will meet a wide variety of people who somehow fall under the label *evangelical*. To adapt a comment famously made by a Supreme Court justice about pornography, "I can't define it, but I know it when I see it."

Over the decades, the emphases of American evangelicals have shifted. Early in the twentieth century, evangelicals tended to define themselves by doctrine, countering theological liberals with an emphasis on the fundamentals of the faith (hence the term *fundamentalism*). In the years following World War II, evangelicals entered an activist phase, founding Bible colleges and universities, dispatching missionaries overseas, and reaching out to a young generation through such organizations as Youth for Christ, Young Life, and Campus Crusade. Evangelicals were often distinguished more by a behavioral lifestyle than by doctrine: "We don't drink, smoke, dance, or chew, and we don't go with girls who do." Later in the century, many of these lifestyle distinctives broke down and the emphasis, in the U.S. at least, moved to politics.

Every few years the national media recognizes the cultural phenomenon. *Time* magazine called 1976, when Jimmy Carter got elected, "the year of the evangelical." During Watergate, Charles Colson attracted much attention for his dramatic born-again conversion. In 2003 Nicholas Kristof wrote an op-ed article in the *New York Times* acknowledging that "nearly all of us in the news business are completely out of touch with a group that includes 46 percent of Americans," the proportion who described themselves in a Gallup poll as evangelical or born-again Christians.

Evangelicalism in the U.S. has become not just a set of beliefs or organizations, but rather a vast subculture that manages to flourish within an increasingly pluralistic culture. In 2003 a book written by evangelical pastor Rick Warren, *The Purpose Driven Life,* sold more copies in a single year than any previous nonfiction book in history. The dozen books in the Left Behind series on the Second Coming of Christ have passed 60 million copies in print. *The Prayer of Jabez* and the older *Late Great Planet Earth* show that blockbuster evangelical books are no fluke. And Mel Gibson's *The Passion of the Christ* stunned Hollywood studios with its success, due in large part to evangelicals' support.

In a tongue-in-cheek article, "What Would Jesus Do?" *GQ* magazine's literary editor Walter Kirn spent a week immersing himself in the evangelical subculture. He read from the Left Behind series, dined on foods recommended in the book *What Would Jesus Eat?,* listened to Christian music on Christian radio stations and on his CD player, shopped at an evangelical bookstore, watched Bibleman videos, and got his news from Christian television and evangelical Internet sites. He even used a computer mouse pad purchased from a Christian store and designed by Thomas Kinkade, Painter of Light. Kirn admitted to some relief from the assaults of secular culture but ended up unimpressed by evangelical subculture: "Ark culture is a bad Xerox of the mainstream, not a truly distinctive or separate achievement. Without the courage to lead, it numbly follows, picking up the major media's scraps and gluing them back together with a cross on top." Yet the very fact that he could spend a week inside that "ark culture" shows its pervasive influence.

The British historian David Bebbington suggests this overall summary of evangelical distinctives, which will be used as a kind of template in this book:

- Conversionism: the belief that lives need to be transformed through a "born-again" experience.
- Activism: the expression of the Gospel in missionary and social reform efforts.
- Biblicism: a particular regard for the Bible as the ultimate authority.
- Crucicentrism: a stress on the sacrifice of Jesus Christ on the cross as making possible the redemption of humanity.

Under this overarching description, Roman Catholics, mainline Protestants, and Orthodox Christians can be evangelicals even while remaining within denominational structures that might shirk the term. The National Association of Evangelicals bars members of the National Council of Churches, and yet many of those denominations have constituents who gladly call themselves evangelicals.

In the interest of full disclosure, I must report that I am an evangelical. I write books for the same publisher that produced *The Purpose Driven Life* (while trying not to envy its sales figures), and I write a monthly column for *Christianity Today,* a leading evangelical magazine. I have spent much of my career within the evangelical subculture, poking around it as a journalist, exploring and sometimes challenging its foibles and eccentricities. As one who emerged out of narrow Southern fundamentalism, I have found the subculture surprisingly broad and diverse. Not once has a magazine or book publisher tried to censor my words.

I studied in the graduate school at Wheaton College, a place that honors and rewards scholarship. I cut my journalistic teeth as editor of *Campus Life,* a magazine published by Youth for Christ, and then served as "editor-at-large" for *Christianity Today.* All three identify themselves strongly with the one person who best exemplifies the evangelical style: Billy Graham, who studied at Wheaton and founded the other two organizations. And all three provided a nurturing environment in which I could work out my own faith, including times of serious doubts and struggles, even as I pressed against the limitations of the subculture. Graham's influence has been enormous: his crusades embraced mainline denominations, Catholics, and charismatics; he dismantled racial barriers; and he eased evangelicals into the public square by addressing such issues as civil rights, abortion, poverty, and the nuclear arms race.

When I mailed the manuscript for *What's So Amazing About Grace?* to the publisher, I told my wife, "This book may get me blackballed by evangelicals." After all, it contained a chapter on Bill Clinton, not exactly a hero to most evangelicals, and a chapter on Mel White, who came out of the closet as a homosexual activist even though he clings to most evangelical theology. I was wrong. Nearly every day I receive an appreciative letter from an evangelical reader.

As a writer, I have found that by sticking to Bebbington's four distinctives, especially his emphasis on the Bible, I have a wide range of freedom. The Bible looms as a decisive self-corrective to the vagaries of evangelical theology and practice. When readers complain, I reply that I am not the radical; Jesus is. He sought out prostitutes and sinners, in the process attracting violent opposition from the religious establishment of his day. He set the standard for personal holiness in the midst of a decadent society while responding with love and grace to the very ones who made it decadent. As he departed, he prayed that his followers would not be removed from the world, charging them instead to live in its midst as salt and light, as representatives of a counterkingdom based on peace and love and justice.

After spending several decades working within evangelicalism I would summarize its essential tenets in three statements:

This is our Father's world. Evangelicals believe that God created the world and lavished it with care. Any residue of goodness on the planet reflects God's "common grace": the sun shines and rain falls both on those who believe and on those who don't. All pleasures, including beauty, sexuality, art, and work, are God's gifts to us, and we look to God's revelation for the pattern in best ordering our desires so that in them we may find fulfillment and not bondage.

Theologian Langdon Gilkey said that if evangelical Christianity has a heresy, it is the omission of God the Father, the creator, preserver, and ruler of all human history and every human community, in favor of Jesus the Son, who is related to individual souls and their destinies. I see his complaint not so much as a heresy as a failure in emphasis. As C. S. Lewis, the patron saint of thoughtful evangelicals, once wrote, "When first things are put first, second things are not suppressed but increased."

As an expression of love for the world, God entered its history (the Incarnation) and gave the Son's life as a sacrifice for its redemption (the Atonement). Its emphasis on Jesus and the cross separates Christianity from all other religions, and evangelicals hold fast to that distinctive. In the mystery of the Trinity, God was "in Christ reconciling the world unto himself" (the Apostle Paul's words). Evangelicals recognize that the world has been invaded by evil, and believe that Christ began a process of reclamation, in which the church plays a crucial role, that will culminate in a final victory.

On one of Karl Barth's visits to Union Seminary, someone asked him what he would say if he met Adolf Hitler. The Swiss theologian replied, "Jesus Christ died for your sins." Evangelicals' emphasis on conversion stems from a profound belief that, as Paul put it, "Christ Jesus came into the world to save sinners; of whom I am chief." Almost every message delivered by evangelist Billy Graham centered on that theme. And yet Graham himself insisted that a stress on getting right with God does not imply a faith "so heavenly minded that it does no earthly good." Quite the contrary. Evangelicals such as William Wilberforce, John Newton, and Charles Simeon in England led the way in social reform.

Sociologists in Latin America have documented how the act of conversion can lead to significant social change. (See, for example, *Base Christian Communities and Social Change in Brazil,* by William Hewitt.) A man goes forward to receive Christ at an evangelistic meeting. He joins a local church, which counsels him to stop getting drunk on weekends. With their help, he does so. He starts showing up at work on Monday mornings, and eventually gets promoted to a foreman position. With new faith and a renewed sense of worth, he stops beating his wife and becomes a better father to his children. Newly empowered, his wife takes a job that allows her to afford education for her children. Multiply that by several score converted citizens, and soon the economic base of the entire village rises.

Through the power of the Spirit, followers of Jesus advance God's kingdom in the world. Karl Barth also said, "To clasp the hands in prayer is the beginning of an uprising against the disorder of the world." Yes, and in recent years evangelicals have increasingly recognized the corresponding need sometimes to unclasp those hands and actively lead the uprising against that disorder.

Evangelical organizations like International Justice Mission fight to liberate victims of sexual slavery even as other missions minister to its victims. Prison Fellowship International visits prisoners and equips them for life outside. Mercy Ships recruits doctors to perform free surgeries in needy countries. Habitat for Humanity pursues the lofty goal of providing suitable housing for whoever lacks it. Organizations such as World Vision, World Relief, Opportunity International, Samaritan's Purse, Food for the Hungry, and World Concern respond to human disasters like plagues, famines, and tsunamis while simultaneously funding development projects to prevent the disasters from recurring. In a reprise of the "settlement movement" a century ago, evangelicals are moving into major cities to establish community-based programs. Belatedly, some evangelical organizations have taken up the cause of the environment. Evangelicals run homeless shelters, addiction programs, and alternative pregnancy centers because they believe such activism helps further God's kingdom in the world, a practical way of answering Jesus' prayer that "they will be done on earth as it is in heaven."

In *The Beliefnet Guide to Evangelical Christianity*, you will meet characters both saintly and eccentric. You will read of dissensions and discord. The history of evangelicalism is a history of humanity, with all its fits and starts. As one who has been nurtured by evangelicalism, I hope you also catch something of the spirit fueling a movement that has proven to be light on its feet, willing to self-correct, and is above all committed to follow Jesus, "who, though he was rich, yet for our sakes became poor, that we, through his poverty, might become rich, and who has left us an example that we should follow in his steps." That last is a goal to which all evangelicals aspire, however falteringly we accomplish it. Without doubt, Jesus is the radical one.

1

Who Are Evangelicals?

I know a man who resigned from his evangelical church as a result of a youth-sponsored coffee house (it was a fund-raiser for a missions trip). The kids were hosting several youth bands, and one of them played that Mick Jagger classic "I Can't Get No Satisfaction." That same night, two middle-aged women who'd grown up on the Stones bobbed, weaved, and clapped hands overhead like something out of Woodstock. They too considered themselves evangelicals. Full disclosure: I was one of those two women.

The point being, as with every mode of religious expression on the American landscape, evangelical Christianity has its contradictions and champions, saints and sinners, workhorses and weirdos. There is not one "bloc" of the American population that fits into a category called evangelicalism. Evangelicals can be white, African-American, Asian, or Hispanic. There are the educated and the uneducated; the rich, the middle, and the underclass; the tax-paying upright citizens; the down-and-out drug addicts and prostitutes; the right-wing conservatives and left-wing liberals. It is better to think of evangelicalism as a river carrying life-giving water to its many branches and streams.

The individuals who inhabit the landscape may come and go. But the river remains, a mystical life force that nourishes otherwise disparate groups and, in a way, holds them together.

When today's inhabitants are gone, the river will do the same for those yet to dwell upon the land.

It can, and does, get messy when a mighty river cuts through the crags of everyday life. For believing evangelicals, the source of the river abides in absolutes. But this results in complications. First, evangelicals themselves do not agree upon the interpretation of these absolutes; and second, they desire so sincerely to obey the mandates of faith that they sometimes take irrevocable stands for or against things with the best of intentions. The man who left the church because of Mick Jagger's song did right by his convictions. The rocking, dancing women expressed God-given delight over great music. In their minds they were responding as King David himself did when the Ark of the Covenant was carried to Jerusalem: Let's rock and roll!

"The lyrics are Augustinian," I later commented to my fellow rocker, upon learning of the man's antipathy. St. Augustine wrote in his *Confessions* (a work widely cited by evangelicals): "You made us for Yourself, and our hearts find no peace until they rest in You." Compare: "I've tried, and I've tried, and I've tried, and I've tried . . . I can't get no satisfaction." In Augustinian terms, Mick Jagger makes perfect sense.

Evangelicals tend to make such justifications. They feel the need to make sense of the culture in theological terms. This can be problematic. The world and even God himself sometimes do not make sense. That is one challenge for evangelicals.

Another challenge is dealing with the negative stereotypes perceived by the public—of evangelicals as right-wing extremists; nerdy Ned Flanders types; sourpuss puffy-haired church ladies; or pasty-faced soft-bellied television Bible thumpers. A survey taken by pollster George Barna in December 2003 noted that Americans generally disliked evangelicals more than any other social sector, except for prostitutes, whom they edged out by only a slight margin. Though true evangelicals wouldn't mind such company (after all, Jesus hung out with prostitutes and other fringe people), one purpose of this book is to clarify contradictions that have aroused public confusion and point out strengths largely undetected in public consciousness.

A few explanations: First, although I employ the masculine pronoun when referring to the Deity and to the Holy Spirit, God possesses no gender (and there are references in the Old Testament where God is likened to a mother). My use of the male pronoun arises from Jesus' description of God as Father, and from evangelicals' use of it to refer to God and the Holy Spirit. Secondly, for the purposes of this book, the two sections of the Bible are denoted as the Old and New Testaments. The former is commonly and rightly known as the Hebrew Scriptures. But evangelicals emphasize a "new covenant" and "new kingdom" inaugurated by Jesus, and look upon the Hebrew Scriptures as Act 1, ultimately fulfilled by Act 2 (the New Testament). The terminology means no disrespect to Judaism, which claims these remarkable writings as their sacred text. Although I have tried to limit my use of insider language, some points cannot be addressed any other way. The reader would be well served to mark the glossary page, as he or she will be turning to it regularly. Finally, I do not presume to speak for all evangelicals in this book. I've consulted many who are knowledgeable in these matters. At the same time, I don't doubt some of what I write will offend and/or be dismissed by others in the evangelical community. I do not intend any offense and regret any that might be taken.

THE BIG QUESTIONS

Nowadays, not all who identify themselves as Christians hold to a specific set of beliefs. In America, the term has even taken on cultural nuances—people who decorate a Christmas tree or eat chocolate bunnies at Easter might think of themselves as Christian, even if they have never been inside a church. Some Islamic countries identify Christianity with satellite-beamed U.S. television shows like *Baywatch*.

Even churchgoing Christians don't all believe the same things. There are three main branches of Christianity: *Catholics*, who recognize the authority of the Pope; *Eastern Orthodox* Christians, who follow an ancient liturgy in worship; and *Protestant* Christians, who reject the authority of the Pope and embrace the Bible as their primary source of inspiration and authority. Evangelicals are Protestants, but not all Protestants are evangelicals.

In a nutshell, evangelicals

- believe they must have a "born-again" experience to become a Christian; many follow their conversion with a public "believer's baptism"; in other cases, however, those who are "born again" have already been baptized as infants.
- emphasize a "personal" relationship with Jesus.

- believe the Bible is historically reliable, and is the best authority for people's lives and relationship with God.
- feel obliged to share their faith in Jesus (which they believe saves them from eternal damnation) with other people, in order to save them, too, from eternal damnation.

Although other Protestants may not object to this approach, many opt for more subtlety. For instance, many Protestants don't emphasize a personal relationship with Jesus or a "born-again" experience, preferring a more gradual approach. They tend to be more private about their faith, and therefore don't share it publicly. They get their inspiration from the Bible by studying the texts—using history, literature, language translation, and archaeology—to figure out what the biblical writers were trying to say. (Despite stereotypes to the contrary, many evangelicals use this approach too—scholarship is not incompatible with the "born-again" experience.)

However, according to evangelicals, the term "Christian" has a very specific meaning. It means claiming Jesus Christ as their champion. They believe that without Jesus' death on the cross, which they see as a sacrifice, union with God is impossible. They also believe that although Jesus died, he rose from death, left them instructions for winning others to life eternal, and then returned to God the Father in heaven. They believe Jesus will return at some future point, and when he does, all will be called to account for their deeds. These beliefs are grounded in the Bible.

IN THE BEGINNING

Evangelicals believe humankind was created by God in the persons of Adam and Eve, and that through them, God imbued humanity with a spark of his image. Therefore, evangelicals believe humans were meant to share harmony with God and enjoy the benefits and abundance of the creation about them. Creation is God's masterpiece, of which human beings are the pinnacle. Many evangelicals do not embrace the theory of evolution, which asserts that human life developed out of lower life-forms. They usually explain the fossil record as perhaps one means God used to advance his creation, though crediting God, not natural selection, for intervening in the process. (This topic is discussed further in Chapter 6.)

As the one and only creator, God held the prerogative as to how this harmony was to play out and laid out a single rule. He said to Adam, "Look! I have given you the seed-bearing plants through the earth and all the fruit trees for your food," and added, "you may eat freely any fruit in the garden except fruit from the tree of the knowledge of good and evil. If you eat of its fruit, you will surely die." This moment in the creation narrative introduces a critical insidious player who, from this point forward, undertakes ruthlessly to ruin people's confidence in God's good purposes. He is Satan, the onetime high angel Lucifer who fell "like lightning" from God's presence, having tried and failed to usurp God's authority.

Evangelicals battle Satan's attempts to sabotage God's plans by preying upon the weakest spot in every human's heart, including (especially) theirs. He started with Eve and Adam, planting the slightest seed of doubt with the simple words: "Did God say . . . ?" Evangelicals believe that from the moment our ancestors doubted God and ate the fruit forbidden to them, so alluringly held out to them by the Great Antagonist, the earth and everything in it fell under Satan's dominion. That is why evangelicals call this moment "the Fall."

Was God powerless to stop his children from making this bad choice? Was he a bad parent? Evangelicals believe he was not powerless, and that he is a good parent. But being a good parent, they believe, compelled God to allow Adam and Eve to make this bad choice. In eating from the one forbidden tree, they dictated their own terms, forfeiting the privilege of intimacy with God and the benefits of the bounty of his creation. Evangelicals say God was willing to risk this failure because he loved his children and wanted their love back freely. To allow for that, he (regrettably) had to open the possibility that his children would choose *not* to love him.

———

Eve and Adam chose not to live according to God's terms, which, evangelicals believe, forged an insuperable breach between them (and their descendants) and God. Just as humans inherited from Adam the spark of God's image, in this rebellious flourish humans likewise inherited the damaged relationship with and alienation from God. This evangelicals call sin—or "missing the intended mark." It is defined in the Book of Common Prayer as "seeking our own will instead of the will of God, thus distorting our relationship with God, with people, and with all creation." The broken bond grieved God, the way any parent would be distressed over a fractured relationship with a son or daughter. Evangelicals believe God effected a plan of restoration and that he executed it by submitting to the terms our ancestors had chosen. He himself entered the situation. He assumed the form of a man in the person of his Son, Jesus.

GOD BECOMES A MAN

Astounding events have been associated with Jesus, as noted in the New Testament. His mother, Mary, became pregnant without "having been with a man." Violent winds grew still at his command. When he willed it, wine flowed out of jars that had held water. Many other extraordinary events occurred during his life that remain difficult to explain apart from an intellectual concession to the miraculous. Evangelicals accept this. They believe that since God, as creator, can manifest molecular arrangements and time sequencing any way he chooses, Jesus as God's physical presence possessed similar capacities.

The reader must note that saying God "assumed the form" of a human being in the person of his Son does not suggest Jesus, at heart, was damaged the way Adam and Eve and their offspring have been. Evangelicals believe Jesus possessed the limitations, emotions, and temptations inherent in being human, but confronted this with his eyes clear, his heart clean, and his step sound. In other words, he was born without original sin.

The saving plan began at the Jordan River. There, to show solidarity with people, Jesus stepped into the muddy river to be baptized by his cousin John, whose baptism symbolized repentance. Thereafter Jesus spoke about a "new kingdom." He told stories that excited some and offended others. He healed many diverse diseases, mental and physical. Increasing numbers rallied around him, mostly down-and-outers, but lawyers and in-

────────────────────── How Come? ──────────────────────

Is "Christ" Jesus' Last Name?

If Jesus had a last name during his years on earth it would have been *bar-Joseph,* son of Joseph. "Christ" is his title, which is Greek for "the anointed one." It is equivalent to the word "Messiah," used in the Old Testament. It became attached to his common name because, as news spread about his life, death, and resurrection, his followers, both Jewish and Gentile, saw him as God's Messiah, or chosen one, who would save God's children from their bondage to sin.

───

tellectuals were also curiously attracted to him. Many were confounded by his teachings. People from all walks of life wanted to learn more about this new kingdom. This swelling group alarmed patriots and the religious establishment, who feared revolt and the unraveling of tradition. This fear, coupled with Jesus' unabashed pronouncements against hypocrisy, turned the cultural and political elite against him. He became ensnared in a web of conspiracy, betrayal, and entrapment that ended badly, as noted in Mel Gibson's *The Passion of the Christ.* "They led him away to be crucified," writes Mark in his Gospel (15:20). Jesus was about age thirty-three.

DID JESUS HAVE TO DIE?

The principle of Jesus' death on the cross as a sacrifice is articulated by evangelicals as "the atonement." Some preachers help listeners understand the notion by breaking it into three small words: *at—one—ment.* By this, they mean Jesus bridged the

chasm between humanity and God by offering his sacrifice as
the means to carry the guilt that (because of the Fall) separated
humanity from God. It is his act of "putting at one" *(at-one-
ment)* a once-fractured relationship, through his willing sacrifice. In the evangelical scheme, this is a mystical transaction,
beyond human understanding. C. S. Lewis, a favorite writer of
evangelicals, says in *Mere Christianity,* "A man can eat his din-
ner without understanding exactly how food nourishes him."
He claims the same could be said of the atonement: "A man
[person] can accept what Christ has done without knowing
how it works: indeed, he certainly would not know it works
until he [or she] has accepted it." Lewis seemed to indicate
that not all believers would agree on how atonement actually
"works." Some say the bad choice of our ancestors demanded
redress because God is holy and justice must be meted out—
and Jesus volunteered to do the job. Another explanation re-
duces the death of Jesus to a moral example of neighborly love
of a type we should rally around as a model (giving up his life
for his friends). The meaning of the atonement lies somewhere
between the two. For evangelicals, it remains a holy mystery.

But isn't living a good life—obeying the Ten Commandments, for example—enough to get right with God? Why do
we have to accept Christ as our personal savior to be "saved"?

Evangelicals would say that even if you don't kill anybody,
things still are not right between you and God. The reason goes
back to the new kingdom Jesus talked about. He said, "You
have heard that the law of Moses says, 'Do not murder' . . . But
I say, if you are angry with someone, you are subject to judgment." Evangelicals conclude that though you might not kill
somebody, you could nevertheless commit murder in your heart

every time your anger flared up. Who can stop feeling anger? The answer is, no one, including evangelicals. This interpretation of the Torah was entirely new in Jesus' time. His teaching took "keeping the Law" to deeper levels that made it impossible for even the religious elite of the time to uphold. Two revolutionary effects ensued, marking the "new kingdom" as well as the "new covenant" that overrode the old: 1) the playing field was leveled so that *no one* could win God's favor by human effort (doing one's religious duty or even living "the good life"), and 2) the concept of *grace* was established (since humans couldn't win it on their own, God rendered his favor as a gift, but only in the salvation bestowed through the coming of his Son).

That is why the restoration (being "saved") could only be realized by the intervention of God himself, through Jesus. He alone could live up to God's standards of humility, honor, holiness, and goodness.

HE ROSE AGAIN

Jesus reiterated repeatedly that he would come back from the dead. According to the Gospels, the day of his death was a Friday. By the time his body was removed for burial, the sun was low and the Sabbath was descending, which meant that his followers, who were observant Jews, were prohibited from finishing the preparation of the body. Sunday morning, when the Sabbath was over, some women, including Mary Magdalene, went to complete the job. They found to their astonishment that the great stone had been removed from the entrance and

the tomb of Jesus was empty. In the devastation after his exe-
cution, his beleaguered followers forgot what he'd said about
his coming back, presumed his body had been stolen, and were
terrified. This moment is the miracle of all miracles according
to evangelical sensibilities. The women at the tomb were spoken to by a shining being they believed to be an angel, who
said, "Do not be surprised. You are looking for Jesus, the
Nazarene, who was crucified. He isn't here! He has been raised
from the dead. Look, this is where they laid his body" (Mark
16:6). He told them to go tell the disciples. Peter and John, two
of Jesus' dearest disciples, raced to the tomb, where they saw
the empty sepulcher for themselves.

THE GREAT COMMISSION

Even more astounding, Jesus appeared to his disciples (and
others) alive after his death. For about forty days, he stayed
with his followers, giving them the mandate to become part of
God's ongoing rescue operation: "Go, and make disciples of all
nations" (Matthew 28:19). He also assured them he would return, and when he did, there would be no more chances for rescue. He commissioned his followers to tell people what he'd
done and to do so before he returned. But he didn't only commission them. He empowered them with the Holy Spirit. He
knew it was going to take grit to pull this off. Before he ascended into the clouds, Jesus instructed them to stay in
Jerusalem until "the Father sends you what he promised. Remember . . . John baptized with water, but in just a few days
you will be baptized with the Holy Spirit. . . . When the Holy

Spirit comes upon you, you will receive power and will tell people about me everywhere—in Jerusalem, throughout Judea, in Samaria, and to the ends of the earth."

———

WHO OR WHAT IS THE HOLY SPIRIT?

Jesus had said, "It is good that I am leaving you [because] . . . the Father [will] send the Counselor as my representative— and by the Counselor I mean the Holy Spirit—he will teach you everything and will remind you of everything I myself have told you."

The Holy Spirit did indeed come, dramatically and bewilderingly, as depicted in the Book of Acts, chapter 2: "On the day of Pentecost, seven weeks after Jesus' resurrection, the believers were meeting together in one place. Suddenly there was a sound from heaven like the roaring of a mighty windstorm in the skies above them. . . . and what looked like flames or tongues of fire appeared and settled on each of them. And everyone present was filled with the Holy Spirit."

The Holy Spirit, for evangelicals, is the invisible presence of God the Father and Jesus the Son who enters the inner lives of believers to teach, guide, console, and empower them in gifts and mission. It is by means of the Holy Spirit in believers that God's rescue operation continues in the millennia following the ministry of Jesus.

How Do God, Jesus, and the Holy Spirit Make "One"?
Evangelicals believe in the Trinity, the word used to describe this inexplicable commingling of God the Father, God the Son, and God the Holy Spirit. The term "the Trinity" does not appear in the Bible, but it was articulated in the same early document that defined the deity of Jesus, the Nicene Creed (A.D. 325). Evangelicals subscribe to the Nicene Creed. The concept of the Trinity asserts that Father, Son, and Holy Spirit perform differing *functions* but share the same *essence,* perhaps the way dihydrogen oxide (water) manifests itself in liquid, solid, and vapor forms, while maintaining the same elemental composition.

WHAT DOES IT MEAN TO BE "BORN AGAIN"?

The notion of being "born again" comes out of an episode in the Gospel of John in which an older Jewish teacher came to Jesus at night (afraid of being seen with him during the day) and probed him about this "new kingdom." Jesus said, "I assure you, unless you are born again, you can never see the Kingdom of God."

The old man was understandably confused. "How can an old man go back into his mother's womb?" he said.

"Humans can reproduce only human life," Jesus said, "but the Holy Spirit gives life from heaven."

Here again, evangelicals debate the nature of this strange transaction. The religious term for being born again is "conversion" (related to repentance), meaning turning around and going in another direction. Some couch it in the catchphrase "choosing Jesus." This is distasteful for many evangelicals, who would say one cannot "choose" Jesus the way one might choose an ice-cream flavor. They would say that in true conversion, Jesus chooses them.

In any case, evangelicals agree that conversion cannot happen apart from the action of the Holy Spirit. In evangelical parlance, the Holy Spirit "readies the heart" ahead of time. Then the moment of turning is a work of the Holy Spirit, a divine action that evokes a change of heart on the inside. For example, a person might begin to feel guilt or hopelessness or become aware of a kind of bondage or fear—the "readying" part of the conversion experience. This, in turn, compels him or her to think about God and perhaps ask God's help. Then, once so focused, God meets the person at his or her point of need through a divine exchange that (as John Wesley described it) "strangely warms the heart." Pascal described it in a single word: "Fire." This "warmed heart" in turn desires a new beginning grounded in a new kind of hope that is focused heavenward, on God. For example, if it belonged to a thief, a newly warmed heart would create in its owner the desire to stop stealing and, in addition, to make up for the damages done because of the wrongdoing. The same could be said of any number of activities or circumstances that might bring on feelings of hopelessness (addiction to drugs or pornography; the loss of a loved one; a life-threatening illness). The looking-up-to-God part is human agency; the "strangely warming" part comes from God. That is why evangelicals call it grace: It is a gift to them freely given by God, without whom the warmth could not be realized.

Perhaps the most famous recent example of the born-again phenomenon is Charles Colson, former White House counsel under President Nixon during the Watergate scandal.

In the late 1960s and early 1970s, Colson was Nixon's "hatchet man," known for political dirty tricks. As recounted in his autobiography *Born Again,* Colson, feeling exhausted, disillusioned, and trapped in the web of Watergate, was truly converted the summer of 1973. But he had made so many enemies and had done so many nasty things that even Christian Republicans didn't believe it.

In 1974 he was charged with obstructing justice. Because God had changed his heart, he stood before the judge and admitted his crime. He walked into the Federal Prison Camp in Montgomery, Alabama, a guilty man and served eight months

---

Evangelical Heroes in Their Own Words

CHARLES COLSON'S BORN-AGAIN EXPERIENCE (FROM *BORN AGAIN*):

Outside in the darkness, the iron grip I'd kept on my emotions began to relax. Tears welled up in my eyes as I groped in the darkness for the right key to start my car. . . . The tears were flowing uncontrollably. There were no streetlights, no moonlight. The car headlights were flooding illumination before my eyes, but I was crying so hard it was more like trying to swim underwater. I pulled to the side of the road . . .

And then I prayed my first real prayer. "God, I don't know how to find You, but I'm going to try! I'm not much the way I am now, but somehow I want to give myself to You." I didn't know who He was. My mind told me it was important to find that out first, to be sure that I knew what I was doing, that I meant it and would stay with it. Only that night, something inside me was urging me to surrender—to what or to whom I did not know.

---

of a one-to-three-year sentence. Today his hugely successful Prison Fellowship Ministries extends to more than six hundred prisons in eighty-eight countries and includes several subsidiary ministries. In other words, after being born again, Chuck Colson stopped his dirty tricks and has tried to compensate for the damage. He became a different man.

WHAT DOES "EVANGELICAL" MEAN?
AND WHY SHOULD PEOPLE BE "SAVED"?

Evangelicals take seriously Jesus' final command to "go and make disciples of all nations, even to the outermost parts of the world." He is telling them to preach the "evangel"—the good news. And the good news is, people still have time before Jesus' return to hear about God's rescue plan and jump in the lifeboat. Evangelicals believe that time is short and that they themselves must answer to God for failing to carry this news to those who might not know it. They carry "the Great Commission" with conviction, believing that all people live in the shadow of Jesus' Second Coming and must seize the opportunity to be saved while it still exists. They often quote the Apostle Paul, who wrote, "For God says, 'At just the right time, I heard you. On the day of salvation, I helped you.' Indeed God is ready to help you right now. Today is the day of salvation" (2 Corinthians 6:2). That is why evangelicals go about trying to "save" people. They are casting a lifeline—the evangel—to humankind in danger of eternal damnation. It is how they came to be called evangelicals.

Beyond bringing about individual conversion, the Holy Spirit also orchestrates a larger plan that demands action of these new people of God. The "true church" spoken of in the

Bible is not a building, such as the term implies today. It arose out of activities of the first believers, who were "sent out" (from the Greek word *ekklesia*, which means "called-out ones"). This new "called-out" band, according to the New Testament, was intended to be a people on the move, not pew sitters in comfortable cushioned seats. Salvation was not rendered so people could join a club; they were saved so they could go out and rescue more people.

Evangelicals don't all agree on how the Spirit manifests himself in the lives of individual believers. It is safe to say, however, they share the common belief that God's presence, through the Holy Spirit, personally and dynamically engages his people in perceivable and sometimes extraordinary ways. He calls them out of comfort zones to go forth. Evangelicals believe that through the Spirit and the people whose hearts he has warmed, God communicates the impulses of his heart and purpose and desires to save as many as will receive him.

That means that members of the church are meant to be action-oriented people, a community on the move. They are the emissaries of Jesus, commissioned to go as Jesus himself had done to live sacrificially, and to share the news about how Jesus made possible a way back to life as God had intended it. To accomplish this, the Spirit empowers people with particular strengths and abilities. One person may be given wisdom; another knowledge; another the ability to heal; another the ability to discern strange spirits. It means that, by the Spirit, believers are strengthened in adversity and given power and great endurance. It means they are able to rejoice in the face of suffering. To quote another evangelical favorite, Martyn Lloyd-Jones, the Spirit can make people embody such joy and courage and assurance "that they [would be] ready to be thrown to the lions."

What's the News?

Evangelicals believe the mysterious actions of God through Jesus were preserved in the testimonies of those who saw the events and documented them. Over the centuries, it became understood that these testimonies were sacred and must be organized and preserved. That is how the New Testament, by the late fourth century, had become a consolidation of narratives about the life of Jesus; the subsequent activities of those who knew him; letters sent around by early believers; and, in the case of the Book of Revelation, a mysterious glimpse into future cosmic events.

Some people assert that the accounts in the New Testament cannot possibly reflect the authentic situation, since the writings were passed down over hundreds of years from scribe to scribe. How can evangelicals put such trust in so precarious a collection of fragmentary documents?

ARE THE BIBLE STORIES TRUE?

Evangelicals' perspective on history supports their belief in the accuracy of the Bible as a whole and the trustworthiness of the New Testament in particular. In the days following his death, the followers of Jesus, all of whom presumably witnessed the same events, checked one another's recollections. The first-century education system depended upon oral recitation and memorization. What little paper they had (made of skins and reeds) was used for public readings and official documents. Those who had been Jesus' closest followers memorized his sayings and remembered his deeds. It didn't take long for these and other followers of Jesus to understand that their mission of telling the world about Jesus ought to be made "official," and therefore written down. They wrote in a common form of Greek, the "street language" of the Roman Empire at the time. (See chapter 6 for some Christian scholars' questioning of the Bible's trustworthiness and for evangelical responses.)

That is not to say that the writings are "objective." The four Gospels for example, which recount the words and works of Jesus, are not intended as biography. If you want to know what Jesus did on his twenty-first birthday, you will not learn that here. The Gospels are proclamations and exist for the single purpose of getting the word out about who Jesus was and why he came to earth. The Gospel writers had an agenda. Mark begins his narrative: "Here begins the good news [Greek: *euangelion*] about Jesus the Messiah."

The events the authors document took place in the public arena and were seen as God himself stepping onto the stage of history. They wrote what they understood to be God's activity, through Jesus, rooted in actual events.

The Gospels focus on the last three years of Jesus' life (with the exception of the birth narratives and a short section in Luke about Jesus at age twelve teaching in the Temple). But the notion of four Gospels would have been alien to the writers' thinking. In their minds there was only one Gospel—one pronouncement—written by four individuals to various com-munities.

Most evangelical scholars (and many outside the evangelical camp) agree the Gospels were written between about A.D. 60 and A.D. 90, and the earliest was the Gospel of Mark. Curiously, Mark was not numbered among the twelve disciples of Jesus. But Jesus had many followers in addition to the twelve who were eyewitnesses to these events. (It was in Mark's parents' home, some believe, that the Last Supper took place.) Matthew, Mark, Luke, and John wrote their books within the lifetimes of men and women who had known Jesus and who, therefore, could have challenged their accuracy. The original biblical writings (probably written on papyrus) have been lost. For the next fourteen centuries, every copy of the Bible was reproduced by hand; today over five thousand ancient New Testament manuscript fragments exist—none of them the same. The earliest fragments date from the second century A.D. The historical proximity of the existing documents to the events they recount gives them enormous weight when it comes to reliability.

However, anyone who has copied a recipe or written down a phone number knows how easy it is to make a mistake in the transmission. When it came to the dissemination of the New Testament texts, errors were made, some inadvertent, some intentional. During the first and second centuries scribes felt it was fine to embellish a document if a reading was difficult, or to "help" readers understand a passage by fixing a discrepancy. It was not until around A.D. 400 that a canonical mentality became entrenched and the free-flowing changes stopped. It should be noted, however, that evangelicals believe no significant teaching or doctrine of the New Testament hinges on an inconsistency in the Gospels.

Since no complete documents exist today, scholars are left to mull over these five-thousand-plus fragments preserved by transcribers, letter by letter. These scholars assume that the documents were transcribed with care. Even so, they recognize the process also involved real people with tired eyes, cramped fingers, and headaches.

This touches on the inerrancy debate, which will be addressed in more detail in chapter 6. In short, biblical inerrancy, for evangelicals, implies that the writings of the Bible—Old and New Testaments—are inspired by God and address historical events that describe God's activity in the world. Evangelicals concede a "shaping process" at the hand of the various authors. But, they believe, the shaping did not introduce fantasy or rewrite history. (For example, no two people witnessing a car accident would describe it identically for the police record; yet the accident actually occurred.) They believe the Bible can be trusted and therefore is authoritative.

WHAT'S WHAT IN THE BIBLE?
Understanding the Old Testament

Evangelicals consider themselves "New Testament" people. How, then, do they understand the Old Testament, a compilation of Jewish writings that evolved over a millennium (1400 to 400 B.C.)?

The Law: The first five books of the Bible are known in Jewish terms as the Torah, or the Law. Therein one finds more than six hundred commands. God's people, the children of Israel, were expected to uphold these as signs of their allegiance to him—their covenant or "terms of agreement." For evangelicals, however, keeping the Old Testament laws is irrelevant as far as terms go, because the Old Testament involved an old covenant, whereas when Jesus came he brought a "new covenant." Taking a cup of wine at the Last Supper, he said: "This is the token of God's new covenant to save you—an agreement sealed with the blood I will pour out for you" (Luke 22:20). The Apostle Paul elaborates: "He is the one who has enabled us to represent his new covenant. This is a covenant, not written of laws, but of the Spirit. The old way ends in death; in the new way, the Holy Spirit gives life" (2 Corinthians 3:6).

Evangelicals receive benefits from reading and meditating on the Old Testament because they believe it offers a paradigm for understanding God: It sets a standard for moral behavior; reflects his care for his people (many of its laws are protective); and shows his merciful nature. The "eye for an eye" dictum is not, as most think, a call for revenge but a demand for restraint: The punishment should equal the crime. For evangelicals, the letter of the law has passed away, but the spirit of the Law abides.

Prophets: The Old Testament prophets are read by evangelicals in the light of Jesus' coming. The people to whom God sent the Law, the nation of Israel, were having a hard time keeping all the rules. As they prospered and grew as a nation, they forgot God's terms and started doing things their own way—robbing the poor, stealing from one another, and worst of all, worshiping idols. The prophets were messengers inspired by God to challenge the nation's bad choices. That is why one sees the words "Thus says the Lord" throughout the prophetic writings. These utterances reminded people of God's original terms and of how they had strayed. At the same time, these writings always included hope: God would yet find a way to reclaim them. In this way, the prophetic books help evangelicals understand four fundamental aspects of God's nature: First, he means what he says; second, if they stray, he comes for them and calls them back; third, if they don't return, judgment will fall; and finally, even when judgment falls, he holds out promise of an ultimate restoration (through Christ).

Historical Narrative: Some of these are legalistic, repetitive, even boring. They don't always work well as "devotional" Bible study because they contain lists, genealogies, and chronologies. Yet historical narratives account for 40 percent of the Old Testament, which makes them a hefty portion of "God's Word." Here again, as in the Gospels, evangelicals view Old Testament historical narratives as *God*'s story—more than "mere" history. They are descriptive accounts of God's activities in creation, in history, and in the individual lives of people—not moral imperatives. For examples, when 2 Chronicles recounts the story of how David saw Bathsheba (a married woman) bathing and then used his position of power to summon her to his bed, evangelicals don't conclude that it's fine for men to use power to manipulate women. However, bad things happened as a result of David's taking Bathsheba into his bed. Thus, evangelicals approach Old Testament historical narratives as a means of understanding God and his dealings with damaged, imperfect people.

Wisdom Literature: The Psalms and other poetic writings (see page 30) are prayers and songs addressed to God from the depth of human emotion. Some, like Psalms 23 and 91, are beautiful meditations on God's protection and power. Others sound sadistic and violent, as when the psalmist, exiled in captivity in Babylon, writes: "Happy is the one who takes your babies and smashes them against rocks" (Psalm 137). Evangelicals recognize this, too, as an example of raw human emotion, in this case a cry of bitter despair from someone "in the depths." Such bitterness is the exception, but evangelicals also use passages like these to cry out to God while staying within the bounds of scripture.

New Testament

Historical Narrative: As noted earlier, the first four books of the New Testament, the Gospels, were intended to be not history (though that element is there) but *good news.* The Book of Acts, which follows the Gospels, was written by the Gospel writer Luke and stands more firmly in the camp of historical narrative. In his Gospel Luke says, "Having carefully investigated all these accounts from the beginning, I have decided to write a careful summary for you, to reassure you of the truth of all you were taught [about Jesus]." In Acts, he continues: "In my first book I told about everything Jesus began to do and teach until the day he ascended to heaven after giving his chosen apostles further instruction from the Holy Spirit." Hereafter, he relates the first movements and expansion of those early believers, the early "church." The focus starts with Peter but midway shifts to Paul. Not only was Paul *not* a follower of Jesus, he was an active persecutor of this new sect. Then Paul encountered Jesus in a mystical vision that knocked him flat on his back and blinded him on a dusty road to Emmaus. This encounter irrevocably changed his life and mission, and from Christianity's enemy he was transformed into its most tenacious champion. By the end of Acts, Paul is imprisoned in Rome, having obeyed the command of Jesus to take his message first to Jerusalem; then Judea and Samaria; and finally to the "outermost parts of the world"—Rome and its empire.

Epistles: The early leaders of this new movement wrote letters, called epistles, to one another and to churches to offer encouragement, thanks for gifts, and exhortations. Most but not all of the letters that appear in the New Testament were written by Paul to people whose lives he had touched with the "good news." Evangelicals have spent a lot of time on Paul's letters, trying to figure out what he was getting at. This is tricky, the equivalent of hearing only one end of a conversation. Many of Paul's letters are written as responses to inquiries received from leaders of churches he had founded in places such as Corinth (in modern-day Greece) or Ephesus (in modern-day Turkey). Often these churches were in turmoil, and the harried overseers had written Paul for advice. What remains are not the inquiries, but Paul's responses.

Evangelicals disagree on many points in Paul's writing. How does one decide, for example, which parts of the letters are divine commands and which are specific to the customs of the age? Some are obvious. Paul tells the believers in Colossae: "Clothe yourself with compassion, kindness, humility and gentleness." Evangelicals agree that is a universal exhortation. But what to do with troubling references from Paul about women being silent in church? Alas, this has proven a divisive issue among evangelicals. An inserted fragment in Paul's letter to the Corinthians says, "I want women to be silent in church." In the same letter, a few chapters earlier, Paul says, "I want the women when they prophesy to wear veils." (Not wearing a veil in public worship back then was interpreted as sexual impropriety.) This poses a conundrum: If women aren't supposed to speak in church, why does Paul concede to their prophesying (albeit with veils)? The only way to resolve this seeming contradiction is to understand that Paul, in this letter, was writing to a specific congregation (in Corinth) that was over the top when it came to certain forms of misconduct in public worship. Women were apparently behaving badly, and he came down hard on them. Seen in this light, both passages (silence and wearing veils while prophesying) actually come together in harmony under the rubric of exhibiting grace, order, and unity in public worship.

Apocalyptic Prophecy: The last and most mysterious book in the Bible is the Revelation of John, filled with horses and dragons, angels and trumpets, earthquakes and lakes of fire, a woman crowned with stars, and a champion in gleaming white. John starts off in a historical vein: "I, John . . . was on the is-

--- How Come? ---

What Do the Numbers Mean in the Bible?

Originally, the Bible was not organized into chapters and verses. The arrangement of the various writings, along with the internal organization of each "book" (broken into chapters and verses), evolved over hundreds of years and was more or less complete by the sixteenth century.

Today, if you were at a baseball game and saw someone holding a sign behind home plate that read "John 3:16," how would you figure out what that sign holder was trying to say?

The reference is to the book of John, chapter 3, verse 16, which reads: "For God so loved the world that he gave his only Son, so that everyone who believes in him will not perish but have eternal life." Once you realized this you would understand that the person holding the sign at the baseball game, rightly or wrongly, was using television cameras to share the *evangelion*, good news.

land of Patmos because of the Word of God and the testimony of Jesus." Once he gets going, however, the text becomes more obscure, full of symbolism and odd sequences. It reflects a genre known as "apocalyptic" literature, a supernatural unveiling of something soon to take place. Apocalyptic literature originated in the Jewish scriptures, especially in the books of Daniel and Ezekiel, and flourished in Palestine through A.D. 100. Apocalyptic writings interpret history as a cosmic struggle between good and evil (in this case, God and Satan), in which history progresses toward a preordained resolution, prior to which evil increases until the "appointed time."

Just as evangelicals understand portions of the Old and New Testaments as revealing a clearer understanding of God and his actions toward his creation, they see Revelation as the "amen" to everything already said. Throughout the Bible, God intervenes in the human arena. The Book of Revelation assures its readers that God in the end will win. The seer—in this case, John—is transported to heaven, where he is shown eternal secrets. He then "returns" to normal consciousness and is left to interpret the vision. In his writing, John seems to reveal the great cosmic forces that lie behind the turmoil of human history. He shows that God, through the return to earth of Jesus, will again break into that history and bring the entire system to a final reckoning. (Chapter 4 examines in depth various "end times" interpretations.)

IS THE BIBLE "THE WORD"?

Evangelicals render devotion to the Bible as "the Word of God." The concept of the Bible as the Word, as it is understood by many evangelicals today, did not, however, exist at the time of Jesus and the early church. Jesus did not carry around a Bible. He *was* the Word, as John's Gospel proclaims in its opening passages: "In the beginning the Word already existed. He was with God and he was God. . . . The Word became human and lived here on earth among us." Jesus himself, as the Word made flesh, manifested God's presence, action, and power. As a Jew he knew by heart the Torah, the Prophets, and the Psalms. He read them devotionally and used them authoritatively. When tempted by Satan in the wilderness (to turn stones into bread), Matthew records Jesus as responding, "The Scriptures say, 'People need more than bread for their life; they must feed on every word of God,' " which comes directly from Deuteronomy 8:3.

Yet the concept of "the Word" as it is understood by evangelicals today has taken on a more rigid application. This is due, in part, to the emphasis laid on the authority of the scriptures during the Protestant Reformation. The temptation among evangelicals has been to put so much emphasis upon scripture's orthodoxy, its ultimate truth, that the writings become a means for drawing theological lines in the sand. Yet these insider arguments should never overshadow the primary purpose of the narratives of the Old and New Testaments—to paint a picture of the greatness of God, and to demonstrate his activity toward the people he created, loves, redeemed, and will ultimately reclaim.

Evangelicals believe the Bible is God's message to humanity. It is their guide for faith and practice—the standard by which human conduct is measured and against which creeds are tested. Most evangelicals also view the scriptures as a source of devotional light to help them draw near to God. Evangelicals attempt this with vigilance. At bottom, they see the Bible as food for the hungry soul.

How Evangelicals Break Down the Bible

OLD TESTAMENT

Historical Narrative

Parts of the Law: Genesis, Exodus, Leviticus, Numbers, Deuteronomy; also Joshua, Judges, Ruth, 1 and 2 Samuel, 1 and 2 Kings, 1 and 2 Chronicles, Ezra, Nehemiah, Esther

Wisdom Literature

Job, Psalms, Proverbs, Ecclesiastes, Song of Songs

Prophets

Isaiah, Jeremiah, Lamentations, Ezekiel, Daniel, Hosea, Joel, Amos, Obadiah, Jonah, Micah, Nahum, Habakkuk, Zephaniah, Haggai, Zechariah, Malachi

NEW TESTAMENT

Proclamation (with some historical narrative)

Matthew, Mark, Luke, John

Historical Narrative

Acts

Epistles (letters)

Romans, 1 and 2 Corinthians, Galatians, Ephesians, Philippians, Colossians, 1 and 2 Thessalonians, 1 and 2 Timothy, Titus, Philemon, Hebrews, James, 1 and 2 Peter, 1, 2, and 3 John, Jude

Apocalyptic Prophecy

Revelation

4

WHO WILL GET LEFT BEHIND?

A dynamic sense about the suddenness of "the end of the world"—called the eschaton—has always served as an animating force in the evangelical mission to save humankind from hell. As historian Paul Boyer wrote, "The most dynamic, energized sector of religion has been the evangelical one, and the eschatological vision is central."

The fascination with end-times prophecy received an enormous boost in the public imagination (and not only among evangelicals) in 1970 with the publication of Hal Lindsey's landmark work *The Late Great Planet Earth,* one of the best-selling nonfiction books of the entire decade. Using Bible prophecies, Lindsey focused on certain events foreshadowing the Second Coming of Christ, which would bring on the Battle of Armageddon and the destruction of the world. Some of the signs, which, as Lindsey pointed out, had been predicted in the Bible, included the founding of the state of Israel, its reclaiming of Jerusalem, conflict in the Middle East, an increase in natural disasters, and a growing interest in witchcraft and Satanism. Still to come, added Lindsey, was the rise of the Antichrist, a powerful individual who would head a one-world government.

Lindsey had the field almost to himself until 1995, when fiction writer Jerry B. Jenkins and Tim LaHaye (one of the founders of the Moral Majority) launched their phenomenally successful Left Behind series of end-times novels. With the publication of the latest installment, *Book Twelve: The Glorious Appearing*, in 2004, total sales of the series reached sixty million copies. That adds up to a lot of people tuned in to "the signs of the times."

From the era of the first Christians, who expected the Lord's return in their lifetime; to the turn of the first millennium, when the whole country of Iceland converted to Christianity out of apocalyptic dread; to the sixteenth-century reformers, who likened the papacy to the Antichrist; to the rise in the 1830s of the Millerites, who waited in vain—twice—for Christ's return; to the predictions of South Korean Lee Jang Rim, who convinced followers around the globe that Christ would return in October 1992—generation upon generation has believed that theirs would be the moment in time when the victorious Savior would return in the clouds to reclaim his people.

The problem is he hasn't.

The result has been inventive reinterpretations about what Christ meant when he spoke of his coming at "the end of the age." Old Testament prophets employed end-times images vividly. Jesus entertained questions about it seriously. Paul reiterated those teachings forcefully. The Book of Revelation depicted these events dramatically. Evangelicals concur that God intended to communicate something about the end of the world. At the same time, they disagree on how to interpret the "signs of the times."

We've already noted that apocalyptic literature, unveiling what happens at the end, originated in the Jewish scriptures and flourished in Palestine through the first century A.D. First-century believers looked for the imminent return of Jesus, fully expecting he would appear before "this generation" passed away (Matthew 24:34). As time went on, they adopted the view that Jesus would return and literally set up a kingdom in Jerusalem, where he would reign for a thousand years. After that, the final judgment would occur.

When it comes to a discussion about the end times, the millennium (one thousand years) crops up frequently. It comes straight out of the Book of Revelation:

> Then I saw thrones, and the people sitting on them had been given the authority to judge. . . . I saw the souls of those who had not worshiped the beast or his statue, nor accepted his mark on their forehead or their hands. They came to life again, and they reigned with Christ for a thousand years. This is the first resurrection [the rest of the dead did not come back to life until the thousand years had ended]. . . . For the second death holds no power, but they will be priests of God and of Christ and will reign with him a thousand years.
>
> (REVELATION 20:4–6)

CALCULATING THE MILLENNIUM

Church thinkers over the centuries have understood these bewildering biblical texts about the Apocalypse in a variety of ways.

In the fourth century, St. Augustine took the notion that Jesus would literally return to set up his kingdom for a thousand-year reign and adapted it to mean that the reign of God was already manifest on earth in "the church" (the community of believers). This interpretation is called postmillennialism, because it infers that the Second Coming of Jesus takes place *after* the thousand-year reign of the church. Thus, Augustine shifted the church's focus from heaven (looking for Jesus to return) to earth (building his kingdom). The church itself was to be the "City of God," the title of one of his principal works. For Augustine, the age between the first Pentecost (when the Holy Spirit gave birth to the church) and the return of Jesus would actually *comprise* the millennium. The epoch would be marked by the ever-increasing influence of the church in overturning evil and making the world ready for the glorious Second Coming. This outlook prevailed for the next fifteen centuries, adapting as time went on to a symbolic understanding of a thousand years rather than a literal one. However, between the Middle Ages and the Protestant Reformation, some came to see the church not as a force to overturn evil but rather an arm of it. Martin Luther, who triggered the Reformation in 1517, considered the office of the papacy to be the Antichrist.

The beliefs of Evangelicals today reflect both these early points of view. American theologians like Jonathan Edwards in the eighteenth century and Charles Finney in the nineteenth century perpetuated Augustine's belief that the church era was itself the millennium and that people would advance in slow, steady steps toward "kingdom fullness." Since the Second Coming of Jesus had long passed the literal thousand-year mark, it came to be accepted as a loosely symbolic scheme, not a literal time sequence. The point was that the church represented the presence of God on earth and thus could advance God's purposes. Charles Finney proclaimed, "If [people] were united all over the world [in evangelistic outreach], the millennium might be brought about in three months."

Yet social hardship and the dominance of the Enlightenment in the early nineteenth century precipitated a spiritual malaise and a decline in the optimistic philosophy of the post-millennials. Political theories such as Marxism emerged, opening the possibility of a secular utopia. At the same time, rationalism overturned revelation. Paul Erb wrote in *The Alpha and the Omega*, "The age of science made biblical eschatology seem like a fairy tale."

A new scheme arose in the early nineteenth century that echoed somewhat the hopefulness of the early church: premillennialism, meaning that the Second Coming would occur *before* the thousand-year kingdom reign, which Jesus and his church would then establish on earth. This theory was laid out by Baptist lay preacher William Miller and found a strong following in the early to mid-1800s. Miller's view fell into disrepute, however, after he and his followers (called Millerites) made two failed attempts to fix the date of Jesus' return. One disappointed follower wrote: "Our fondest hopes and expectations were blasted, and such a spirit of weeping came over us as I never experienced before." By the mid-1800s premillennialism had, as one historian put it, "fallen on hard times."

It found new life in the late 1850s under the British pastor John Nelson Darby, whose complicated system was called *dispensational* premillennialism. According to Darby, God acted in a series of epochs, or dispensations. The Bible addressed the past and the future, but remained silent about the present age (what Darby called "the great parenthesis"). The next epoch—whenever it would occur—was to begin at the time of the "Rapture," the snatching away of the believing church out of the world (the scenario so graphically depicted in the Left Behind series. This would set in motion subsequent events, culminating in the rise of the Antichrist (Satan's henchman), who would rule the world for seven years. At that time, Jesus would return from heaven with his followers and end Satan's dominion over

──────────────── How Come? ────────────────

Are We Living in the End Times?

Some say yes, referring to correspondences between biblical prophecy and modern events, including:

- "The secret power of lawlessness" (2 Thess. 2)—Terrorism and the accumulation of unauthorized biological, chemical, and nuclear weapon by terrorist groups.
- "Buying and selling" (Rev. 13)—The World Trade Organization.
- "Increase of knowledge" (Dan. 12)—Technological global networking.
- The Jewish people are restored to Israel (Jer. 30:1–3; Ezek. 34:11–24; Zech. 10:6–10)—The founding of the State of Israel in 1948.
- The fall of Babylon (Isa. 21:9; Rev. 14:8)—The ousting of Saddam from Iraq, where the city of Babylon is located on the Euphrates River.
- The uniting of ten kingdoms, the revival of the Roman Empire (Dan. 7:24)—The creation of the European Union and the Common Market.

But such speculations antagonize some evangelicals. Wheaton College professor Mark Noll writes in his book *The Scandal of the Evangelical Mind* that modern-day end-times prophets tend to be "blown about by every wind of apocalyptic speculation" and "enslaved to the cruder spirits of populist science."

earth, defeating him at the battle of Armageddon (a valley in Israel). This victory would inaugurate the thousand-year reign during which the Lord and his church would enjoy uninterrupted bliss, and Israel would experience spiritual rebirth. Satan would be "loosed" for a short season at the end of the millennium (Revelation, cited above). Then heaven and earth would give way to a new heaven and a new earth. Final judgment would commence: some would be welcomed to God's presence for eternity, others condemned to his eternal absence. Satan would be cast into eternal damnation.

"Darby wove these diverse strands into a tight, cohesive system that he buttressed at every point by copious biblical proof texts, then tirelessly promoted through his writing and preaching tours," writes Paul Boyer. Cyrus Scofield popularized this system with the publication of his Reference Bible (1909) and introduced it into the Protestant mainstream.

NO AGREEMENT

There has been no consensus on these scenarios among evangelicals. For example, scholars debate whether Jesus' words about cataclysmic events that usher in the end times refer to the destruction of Jerusalem by the Romans, which occurred in A.D. 70, or to the end of all history in the future. Paul's meaning in his description of "the coming of our Lord" in 2 Thessalonians evokes similar disagreement. Interpreting the Book of Revelation is yet more complicated. Some argue the book can be understood only as a "tract for hard times" aimed at suffering first-century Christians. Others suggest that the Book of Revelation is a symbolic portrayal of the history of the church from its birth at Pentecost to its consummation at the return of Jesus. Another group, called the "Idealists," interprets Revelation in symbolic terms, with imagery such as the red dragon and the woman crowned with twelve stars allegorically representing the cosmic battle between evil and the kingdom of God. And the "Futurists" see Revelation largely as literal prophecy yet to be fulfilled.

There are problems and shortcomings with all of these scenarios. If it is all so muddled and indeterminable, how then do evangelicals claim to know anything at all about these mysterious passages that compose so significant a portion of the New Testament?

JESUS FORETELLS THE FUTURE

The disciples of Jesus asked him, "What will be the sign of your coming and of the end of the age?" (Matthew 24:3). He took plenty of time to answer. The "signs" he enumerated included things like wars, rumors of wars, famines, and earthquakes. He interspersed his answer with warnings that his followers would be persecuted and false messiahs would attempt to deceive even the elect. He spared no force of imagery in describing the severity of the events preceding "the end." ("The sun will be darkened, and the moon will not give its light; the stars will fall from heaven, and the powers of heaven will be shaken" (Matthew 24:29).

He reinforced these admonitions with parables his hearers would understand: The signs preceding his coming, he said, would be as clear as new leaves on a fig tree signaling the approach of summer. His arrival would be swift and sure. It would intrude upon everyday life, but only God knew the precise time. Just as in the parable of the owner of the house (Matthew 24:43), the followers of Jesus are told to expect the unexpected. In the parable of the ten virgins (Matthew 25:1–13) they are cautioned against negligence: Only the five wise virgins had their lamps trimmed and ready when the bridegroom finally arrived, while the five foolish ones were shut out. Similarly, in the parable of the "talents" (ancient coins) in Matthew 25:14–30, the enterprising servants who multiplied the gifts left in their care won their master's reward. By contrast, the lazy "worthless servant" buried his gift and suffered his master's punishment (being "thrown into outer darkness, where there will be weeping and gnashing of teeth").

Jesus prefaced his end-times narrative with the warning to "watch out that no one deceives you." He warned his disciples to be awake, alert, and ready, and not to give up if events took longer than they expected. Jesus' surest prediction of the coming of the end was, however, "No one knows about the day or the hour."

READY TO GO AND READY TO WAIT

How then do evangelicals remain poised to go, yet resigned to wait? Again, they turn to the Bible for answers. In 2 Peter 3, the Apostle Peter writes that scoffers will say, "Ever since our fathers died, everything goes on as it has since the beginning of creation. . . . Where is this 'coming' he promised?" Yet Peter reminds his readers that Jesus' delay only means more hope for more people. Peter exhorts them: "You ought to live holy and godly lives as you look forward to the day of God . . . looking forward to a new heaven and a new earth." But what about the meantime?

Evangelicals find themselves suspended between two seemingly contradictory realities. On the one hand, they try to be "ready to go" and unattached to false promises of worldly acclaim. On the other hand, they are exhorted to live fully, here and now, "making the most of their time" with assurance and hopefulness. Both dispositions depend upon faith in God's unseen promises.

Evangelicals, living in the shadow of the end, have sometimes been preoccupied with lesser questions about where the Antichrist lives or what country won't be destroyed in Armageddon (the kinds of questions Hal Lindsey tackled in *The Late Great Planet Earth* and its publishing offspring). But most concur that the greater question to examine was asked by Jesus himself: "When the Son of Man comes, will he find faith on earth?"

Jesus' verdict in his end-times discourse emphasizes the imperatives of service and action in the present. He concluded with the parable of the sheep and the goats: "When the Son of Man comes in his glory . . . all the nations will be gathered in his presence, and he will separate them as a shepherd separates the sheep from the goats" (Matthew 25:31–33). We will be judged, he says, by the day-to-day actions performed in his name—not based upon speculative interpretations and timetables, but on whether his people extended a glass of cold water to "one of the least of these." Evangelicals then are called to live as if each day were the last. At the same time, each day is born with new promise. Living in the shadow of the end beckons them to invest each moment with service and fearlessness. In so doing, they are investing in the promise of God.

Does God Send Good People to Hell?

That depends on what one means by "good." If being good or bad were the determining factor of one's eternal destiny, the Apostle Paul would be burning in hell for supporting the murder of Christians before he converted, and King David would be right there with him (he ordered the death of one of his soldiers to cover his affair with the soldier's wife). For evangelicals, human definitions of goodness and badness are not criteria for getting into heaven. They cite Paul's letter to the Ephesians: "Salvation is not a reward for the good things we have done, so none of us can boast about it." Hell is a certain destination for all who reject Jesus and his offer of salvation, even if they do good in their lives.

The reality of hell cannot be dismissed, according to evangelicals, if one believes Jesus' own words. "How will you escape the judgments of hell?" he asked the Pharisees (Matthew 23:33). He warned that in the end times the true worshipers would be separated from the hypocrites, who would be told: "Away with you, you cursed ones, into the eternal fire prepared for the Devil and his demons!" (Matthew 25:41).

Evangelicals say that everyone who makes it to heaven gets there by virtue of the blood of Christ. They reject "universalism," the idea that no one is consigned to hell or that good people who reject God and his Son will get to heaven anyway. Old Testament figures, like Moses, David, and Elijah, who existed before Jesus, are considered to have been "saved by faith"—a faith that looked forward to the Messiah.

What is the fate of the millions of souls who, through no fault of their own, have never been privy to the good news or of the children who die before they can understand such things? How God employs Jesus' salvation and at what point it is rendered is a mystery beyond human reckoning, evangelicals believe. This is best left in the hands of God, who determines eternal destinies. However, evangelicals believe that people today who have the benefit of knowing the good news must share it. And those who have been exposed to the Gospel will answer for whether they accept or reject it.

Paul puts it this way: "Anyone who calls on the name of the Lord will be saved. But how can they call on him to save them unless they believe in him? And how can they believe in him if they have never heard about him? And how can they hear about him unless someone tells them? And how will anyone go and tell them without being sent? . . . faith comes from listening to this message . . . the Good News about Christ" (Romans 10:13–15, 17).

5

Historical Forebears

The Roman emperor Nero (A.D. 54 to 68) publicly executed many of the first Christians, including Peter and Paul. Even so, by end of the second century this new sect had made its way throughout all provinces of the empire and into Mesopotamia (modern-day Iraq). The visionary and frontier spirit has been woven into evangelical sensibilities from the time Jesus commanded his followers to "go and make disciples of all nations."

In A.D. 303, however, growth of the movement came to a halt, when the emperor Diocletian ordered an edict of persecution against Christians, who were hunted, tortured, and killed. Those who survived lived in caves and tunnels, or in sanctuaries chiseled out of hollow cliffs. Some of these are still visible today in parts of Italy, Turkey, and other areas that formerly composed the Roman Empire.

The picture changed in A.D. 311 when the emperor Constantine came to power. A convert to Christianity, he reversed Diocletian's policy of persecution. Over time "converting" was viewed favorably, and increasingly people "made confessions" of Christian belief simply for the status it rendered.

This was a complicated time in history generally, and more so for the church. By the fourth century, the Roman Empire was in serious decline. It finally fell in A.D. 431 to invading barbarians, whom the Romans could not effectively resist because of internal decay and general complacency. At the same time, Constantine's edict had rendered the church the luxury of freedom to reflect and debate the nature of its beliefs. This resulted in the emergence of what were considered spurious teachings (called heresies), particularly about Jesus. Among these were beliefs that Jesus had been only human, not divine, as well as the opposite—that Jesus had been only divine and not human. The competing ideas about Jesus were creating confusion. So church leaders decided to define Christianity's beliefs more cogently. The leaders gathered at Nicaea in modern-day Turkey in A.D. 325 and fashioned the Nicene Creed, which clarified the nature of Jesus and outlined the doctrine of the Trinity (see page 14). The Council of Nicaea changed the church's emphasis from general proclamation of the good news about Jesus to the teaching and study of doctrine.

A brilliant theologian of the time, Augustine, bishop of Hippo (a center of learning in northern Africa under Roman rule), came up with a different concept of the church—he conceived of it as the City of God here on earth, rather than a fu-

---

AUGUSTINE OF HIPPO

Now at last, tired of being misled, entrust to the Truth all that the Truth has given to you and nothing will be lost. All that is withered in you will be made to thrive again. All your sickness will be healed. Your mortal body will be refashioned and renewed and firmly bound to you. . . . My soul, why do you face about and follow the lead of the flesh? Turn forward, and let it follow you.

(Confessions)

---

ture place in heaven. In addition, Augustine introduced the idea of public confession of sin. An example of this is found in his autobiography, *Confessions*: "I acknowledge that it was by your grace and mercy that you melted away my sins like ice." Augustine also gave concrete expression to the concept of original sin. If the Nicene council created a doctrine, Augustine gave it a human face. He declared his own bondage to sin and his helplessness to save himself, except through the supernatural grace of the God-Man Jesus.

Bishops like Augustine continued to gain in authority, while the democracy that had characterized the early church waned. In the meantime, under the barbarian onslaught, the Roman Empire finally fell a year after Augustine's death in 430.

THE REFORMATION

By the Middle Ages the church hierarchy had become wealthy, powerful—and corrupt. In the 1100s and 1200s, for instance, Catholic clergy were known to carry on openly with concubines and even solicited the Pope's opinion as to whether keeping multiple mistresses constituted polygamy. (There were exceptions, such as Francis of Assisi.)

But things began to change on October 31, 1517, in Wittenberg, Germany, when a fiery, independent-minded Catholic priest named Martin Luther tacked up a notice on the door of a church. He might as well have taken a sledgehammer to the papal throne. Luther posted what are called his 95 Theses, which were the medieval equivalent of "95 Ways You're Being Fooled by the Church."

Luther's intention was to excite some debate. He instead triggered the single most revolutionary event in church history: the Protestant Reformation. Luther and a collection of thinkers and scholars ended up orchestrating what became a new movement apart from the Catholic Church. Two of Luther's principal ideas have become the hallmark of evangelical theology today: they are the concepts of "justification by faith" and *sola scriptura*.

MARTIN LUTHER'S EPIPHANY

Luther taught theology at the University of Wittenberg and was lecturing on the Psalms when a turning point occurred. He read in Psalm 22 "My God, my God, why have you forsaken me?"—words Jesus himself was said to have uttered on the cross. This awakened him to a new understanding of God, a moment of enlightenment that the late Reformation historian Roland Bainton tried to capture: "What could this mean? Forsaken, abandoned, alienated and estranged from God? . . . Christ had experienced all this too, but why? . . . God is pure, man is impure. God is strong, man is weak. But Christ was not impure, Christ was not weak. Why then was he forsaken?" (*The Reformation of the Sixteenth Century*)

That is the moment in which Luther comprehended the meaning of grace. He understood suddenly that an all-powerful God had made himself powerless by becoming a man, whose sacrifice carried the weight of all sadness, loss, betrayals, cruelties, and tragedies that resulted from Adam's one bad decision in the garden of Eden. This moment underlies the reason why evangelicals would later pray "in Jesus' name" and why they would declare "Jesus saves." They desire such salvation for everyone who believes in God's miraculous rescue through Jesus.

Luther then experienced the second aspect of his inner revolution: the life-altering effect of reading the Bible. He came to believe that only by studying, meditating on, and praying directly and personally through the scriptures can an individual awaken to God. This meant that the Bible ought to be made available to all believers, not imparted in Latin by church officials. Luther was the first to translate the Bible into German for ordinary people to read.

MARTIN LUTHER

Thus this gospel of God or New Testament is a good story and report, sounded forth into all the world by the apostles, telling of a true David who strove with sin, death, and the devil, and overcame them, and thereby rescued all those who were captive in sin, afflicted with death, and overpowered by the devil. Without any merit of their own he made them righteous, gave them life, and saved them, so that they were given peace and brought back to God.

(Preface to the New Testament)

RIPPLE EFFECTS

The rest of the Reformation—with no disrespect to church historians—is comprised of variations on a theme. John Calvin (1509–1564) is second to Luther in his influence on contemporary evangelicalism. As a young Frenchman, Calvin was influenced by Luther's writings and those of another reformer, Ulrich Zwingli. At the age of twenty-three, Calvin published the first of what became a voluminous collection of theological writings known as *Institutes of the Christian Religion.* If Luther hammered away at papal corruption, Calvin chiseled detail into Christian teaching. In essence, he followed the Augustinian message: Humanity was corrupt by nature because of Adam's rebellion, and powerless to overcome its corruption. The uniquely "Calvinistic" edges he carved into emerging Protestantism expanded into notions of predestination and election.

In short, these concepts mean that some individuals—the "elect"—have been preordained to come to God through no

---

JOHN CALVIN

First, human will does not by liberty obtain grace, but by grace obtains liberty. Secondly, by means of the same grace, the heart, being impressed with a feeling of delight, is trained to persevere, and strengthened with invincible fortitude. Thirdly, while grace governs the will, it never falls; but when grace abandons it, it falls forthwith. Fourthly, by the free mercy of God, the will is turned to good, and when turned, perseveres. Fifthly, the direction of the will to good, and its constancy after being so directed, depend entirely on the will of God, and not on any human merit. Thus the will (free will, if you choose to call it so), which is left to man, is, as he in another place describes it, a will which can neither be turned to God, nor continue in God, unless by grace; a will which, whatever its ability may be, derives all that ability from grace.

(The Institutes, Book II)

---

merit of their own, but through God's all-knowing purposes. This teaching caused some to conclude Calvinism (as it came to be called) diminished the evangelical mandate to "go" and "save" (if one is predestined to be the elect, why bother?). Calvinists disagree, however, saying that no one knows whom God has chosen and the means through which his elect might be saved. As a result, they say, every Christian must undertake evangelistic mission. Two other offshoots of the Reformation left an imprint on contemporary evangelicalism. These are the Anabaptists and the Pietists.

The term "Anabaptist" comes from the Greek, and means "baptize again." Anabaptists upheld the notion that baptism should be reserved not for infants (as Luther and Calvin both affirmed) but only for those who were old enough to profess their faith. Anabaptists eschewed violence (they would not participate in the military); banned unbaptized churchgoers from the Lord's Supper (what other Christians call Communion); and refused to take oaths. They were fiercely persecuted by the Calvinists, especially in Geneva, but made a strong impact on subsequent Protestant groups, such as the Baptists.

A century after Luther's Reformation, Pietism arose in Germany, primarily in the teachings of Philip Jakob Spener. Pietists believed that Lutheranism had become dead the same way Luther had said the Catholic Church was dead. Pietists emphasized personal devotion through joyful service to others and similarly emphasized the authority of the Bible. Where Lutheranism and Calvinism were absorbed with doctrinal housekeeping, the Pietists took relational and evangelistic zeal to new levels. They were do-gooders. They were also *be*-gooders, striving through personal devotion to "do what Jesus would do" at all times.

PHILIP JAKOB SPENER

Let us not abandon all hope before we have set our hands to the task. Let us not lay down our rod and staff if we do not have the desired success at once. What is impossible for men remains possible for God. Eventually, God's hour must come, if only we wait for it. Our fruit, like other fruit, must be borne in patience, and the fruit of others must be cultivated by us with perseverance.

(Pia Desiderata [Pious Wishes])

THE CITY ON A HILL: THE PURITANS

The Protestant Reformation in Europe made its way to American soil by way of the British—first on the *Mayflower* and later through John Wesley, George Whitefield, and others. At the time of the Protestant Reformation, England's King Henry VIII (1509–1547) abolished Catholicism as the official church of the government and installed himself as head of the Church

---

JOHN WESLEY

If you have at any time thought, spoken, or acted wrong, be not backward to acknowledge it. Never dream that this will hurt the cause of God; no, it will further it. Be therefore open and frank when you are taxed with anything; do not seek either to evade or disguise it; but let it appear just as it is, and you will thereby not hinder but adorn the Gospel.

(A Plain Account of Christian Perfection)

---

of England, known as the Anglican Church. (In the United States it is called the Episcopal Church.) Subsequent rulers on the British throne teetered one way then another in a tug-of-war over which form of Christianity would win: Anglican Protestantism or Roman Catholicism.

By the early 1600s, a separatist group felt strongly that any hint of Catholicism in the Protestant faith, even with an Anglican expression (which retained many trappings of Catholicism), ought to be rejected. They set out to purify the Church of England, and that is how they became known as Puritans. King James I (of the famed King James Bible of 1611) condemned the "Popish Canons, Courts, Classes, Customs" and other remnants of Catholicism but nevertheless remained loyal to the Church of England. He said of dissenters like the Puritans, "I will harry them out of the land, or else worse."

Thus warned, a group of Puritans fled to Holland. Unhappy there, they decided to leave for the new world across the sea, hoping to re-create English culture there. On September 6, 1620, some one hundred of them sailed from Plymouth, England, intending to reach the already established territory of the Virginia Company. They missed it by forty-one degrees latitude, landing instead on desolate shores farther north, in today's Cape Cod, Massachusetts. They named the spot Plymouth and soon began to establish the settlement as God's Holy Commonwealth.

More like-minded English separatists followed the so-called Pilgrim Fathers. In 1630, John Winthrop brought over six hundred pilgrims (and served as the settlement's first governor). In a famous sermon, he called this "new" England, a "city upon a hill." The sermon, "A Model of Christian Charity," established the ethos for this religious experiment, which has left its mark on the American consciousness. He preached that the only way to avoid calamity in this new land was to adopt the standard set by the Old Testament prophet Micah: "to do justly, to love mercy, to walk humbly with our God. For this end we must be knit together in this work as one man. . . . We must consider that we shall be as a city upon a hill, the eyes of all people are upon us."

The Puritans left England to establish a New Testament model of worship and civic life. They also believed education was integral to their governance. Within the first ten years of their settlement in New England, they established Harvard College as an institution for training ministers.

DENOMINATIONAL STREAMS AFTER THE PROTESTANT REFORMATION				
From: **Luther**	**Calvin**	**Anabaptists**	**Pietists**	**Church of England (Anglican)**
Lutheran	Presbyterian	Quaker	Moravian	Episcopalian
	Reformed	Baptist	Methodist	
	(Puritans)	Mennonite		

OTHER INFLUENCES ON THE FRONTIER

Puritan sensibilities were not the only influences that made their way to the American frontier. By the 1700s, developments in the natural sciences and philosophy enormously enlarged skepticism about the Christian definition of the cosmos. All areas of thought and human engagement were affected by the wave of Enlightenment humanism. Adam Smith introduced laissez-faire economics. The French philosopher Voltaire challenged the notion of an intimate God, viewing him as aloof and disinterested. David Hume questioned miracles, asserting that anything not derived from physical evidence was fantasy. Harvard, once a beacon of evangelical intellectualism, became its antagonist. The Enlightenment put human reason above the wisdom and unknowable aspects of God, asserting that only what could be seen was truth.

Evangelicalism might have faded in the eighteenth and nineteenth centuries were it not for a phenomenon that is as difficult to describe as it is to explain. During this period evangelical Protestants experienced what are called the Great Awakenings. The first ignited in England under John Wesley, then spread to New England under the preaching of British Anglican evangelical George Whitefield and American Jonathan Edwards (among others). The second Awakening, in the nineteenth century, was fueled by Charles Finney. These preachers aroused spiritual anxiety in masses of people, driving them to repent and convert. The awakenings had an enormous impact on evangelicalism today.

THE FIRST AWAKENING

Jonathan Edwards has been pegged as a hellfire preacher for his sermon "Sinners in the Hands of an Angry God." But that does him injustice; he was also one of America's greatest intellectuals. He lived in Northampton, Massachusetts, serving his grandfather's small parish. He preached in a dry manner, his eyes fixed on the pull rope of the church bell at the rear of the meetinghouse, according to a contemporary observer. Thus he was astonished when his sermons started stirring people's hearts. Some even began falling out of their pew boxes into the aisle, overcome with the desire to repent. As Edwards wrote in his 1742 book *Some Thoughts Concerning the Present Revival of Religion*:

> Multitudes in all parts of the land, of vain, thoughtless, regardless persons, are quite changed, and become serious and considerate. There is a vast increase of concern for the salvation of the precious soul and of that inquiry, What shall I do to be saved? The hearts of multitudes had been greatly taken off from the things of the world, its profits, pleasures, and honors. Multitudes in all parts have had their consciences awakened, and have been made sensible of the pernicious nature and consequences of sin, and what a dreadful thing it is to be under guilt and the displeasure of God, and to live without peace and reconciliation with him. They have also been awakened to the sense of the shortness and uncertainty of life, and the reality of another world and future judgment, and of the necessity of an interest in Christ.

Charles Finney (1792–1875) emerged in the 1800s with a different kind of revival, which became known as the Second Great Awakening. Whereas Edwards saw the phenomenon of religious awakening as a movement of God alone, apart from human agency, Finney believed that religious revivals could be generated with "a right use of constituted means." For example, Finney advised that if people placed ads in newspapers, had ministers and laypeople on "the anxious bench" to receive and counsel the converted, and played music to set the mood, the stage would be set for the Spirit to allow revival to happen. Finney changed the emphasis of evangelical revival from God-prompted to human-sponsored. He was the father of "crusade

THE **TWO SIDES** OF JONATHAN EDWARDS

Your wickedness makes you as it were heavy as lead, and to tend downwards with great weight and pressure towards hell; and if God should let you go, you would immediately sink and swiftly descend and plunge into the bottomless gulf. . . . Thus all you that never passed under a great change of heart, by the mighty power of the Spirit of God upon your souls; all you that were never born again, and made new creatures, and raised from being dead in sin, to a state of new, and before altogether inexperienced, light and life, are in the hands of an angry God.

(Sinners in the Hands of an Angry God)

In some, converting light is like a glorious brightness suddenly shining upon a person, and all around him: they are in a remarkable manner brought out of darkness into marvelous light. In many others it has been like dawning of the day, when at first but a little light appears, and it may be presently hid with a cloud; and then it appears again, and shines a little brighter, and gradually increases, with intervening darkness, till at length it breaks forth more clearly from behind the clouds.

*(A Faithful Narrative of the
Surprising Work of God)*

evangelism," moving about the American frontier and gathering crowds to hear him preach. (The Billy Graham Evangelistic Association follows this model.)

SOCIAL CONSCIOUSNESS

These awakenings did more than make people fall into church aisles or prompt them to "come forward" at an altar call. They also imbued evangelicalism with a strong social and missionary impulse. The quintessential model of this approach to evangelicalism arose, again, in England, in the person of William Wilberforce (1759–1833). He is credited with nearly single-handedly taking on and overturning the most financially profitable and morally reprehensible institution of contemporary Britain—the slave trade. He wrote in his diary: "In the Scripture, no national crime is condemned so frequently and few so strongly as oppression and cruelty, and the not using our best endeavors to deliver our fellow creatures from them." His crusade lasted more than four decades, during which he faced opposition from business interests, politicians, racial bigots, and foreign government and public apathy. He was the object of personal assault and contended with failing health.

Wilberforce's father died when the boy was nine, and his mother sent him to live with relatives who, it turned out, were friends of the renowned circuit evangelist George Whitefield. The young Wilberforce was exposed not only to his preaching but also to that of the reformed slave trader John Newton (author of the hymn "Amazing Grace"), who became a father figure to him. However, his mother feared the influence of "Methodist religion" on her son and brought him back home.

A man of personal charm and indomitable spirit, Wilberforce won a seat in Parliament in 1780 at the age of twenty-one. He would remain there for the next forty-five years. At one time he was tempted to withdraw from public life, but was convinced by his good friend William Pitt, then England's prime minister, that his public platform was the gift of God. Later Wilberforce

> ### WILLIAM WILBERFORCE
>
> I wish you from my heart not to become a Politician. I hope you will act on a far higher level and where the path blessed by God is clearer as well as more peaceable.
>
> *(Advice to his son Robert at Oxford)*

wrote in his diary, "My walk is a public one. My business is in the world, and I must mix in the assemblies of men or quit that which Providence seems to have assigned me."

His persistence paid off in 1807 when the abolition of slavery was secured politically, though not realized in full for another twenty-six years. In that year, 1833, Wilberforce died on the very night the House of Commons passed the Act of Emancipation.

Wilberforce's influence was profound. He awakened the social conscience of many evangelicals, including William and Catherine Booth, who founded the Salvation Army in Britain in 1865 with the purpose of reaching the urban underclass in slums. Their success was so overwhelming the movement spread beyond England's shores, reaching the U.S. in the early 1880s. Directly inspired by the example of Wilberforce, William Booth wrote in his book *In Darkest England and the Way Out* (1890):

> Often and often, when I have seen the young and the poor and the helpless go down before my eyes into the morass, trampled underfoot by beasts of prey in human shape that haunt these regions, it seemed as if God were no longer in His world but that in His stead reigned a fiend, merciless as Hell, ruthless as the grave. Hard it is

to read in Stanley's pages of the slave-traders coldly arranging for the surprise of a village, the capture of the inhabitants, the massacre of those who resist, and the violation of all the women; but the stony streets of London, if they could speak, would tell of tragedies as awful, of ruin as complete, of ravishments as horrible.

Evangelicalism's movement outward—of "going" and "reaching" those without benefit of the Gospel—intensified in the nineteenth century, in what has become known as "the golden age of missions." It is worth noting that this effort was fueled largely by women. Whether by nature or default, women's work in urban centers and across the seas focused on the tangible and relational aspect of the Gospel message. They fed and clothed the poor, emphasized education, served as medical missionaries, helped orphans, and taught the Bible. By the late nineteenth century, more women than men filled the missionary ranks. Women themselves formed an informal network called the "women's missionary movement," which helped develop more than forty-five women's agencies (independent and denominational) that mobilized women. One of these women, Mary Slessor, inspired

---

CATHERINE BOOTH

If [a woman] has the necessary gifts, and feels herself called by the Spirit to preach, there is not a single word in the whole book of God to restrain her, but many, very many, to urge her and encourage her.

(Female Ministry; Or, Woman's Right to Preach the Gospel)

David Livingston to devote his life to mapping then-uncharted inland Africa. Slessor had been a Scottish Presbyterian mine worker when, in 1876 at age twenty-seven, she went to Africa, reaching the interior of Calabar (present-day Nigeria), which her male predecessors had been unable to penetrate. She remained there for thirty-eight years as a circuit preacher.

Other pioneering women included Lucretia Mott, who in 1833 helped found the Philadelphia Female Anti-Slavery Society; Fanny Crosby, who, though blind, began a New York inner-city mission in 1880; and Amy Carmichael who, in the early 1900s, rescued child prostitutes in India.

By the end of the 1800s, Enlightenment humanism had sown its seeds. Protestantism generally, and evangelicalism specifically, had met its match. The late nineteenth and early twentieth centuries saw the beginning of another kind of revolution that would carry devastating results for evangelicalism and leave the movement in an entrenched defensive position for half a century.

DWIGHT L. MOODY

We are told to let our light shine, and if it does, we won't need to tell anybody it does. Lighthouses don't fire cannons to call attention to their shining—they just shine.

(Misc. writings)

The Nicene Creed

We believe in one God, the Father, the Almighty, maker of heaven and earth, of all that is, seen and unseen.

We believe in one Lord, Jesus Christ, the only Son of God, eternally begotten of the Father, God from God, Light from Light, true God from true God, begotten not made, of one Being with the Father. Through him all things were made. For us and for our salvation he came down from heaven: by the power of the Holy Spirit he became incarnate from the Virgin Mary, and was made man. For our sake he was crucified under Pontius Pilate; he suffered death and was buried. On the third day he rose again in accordance with the Scriptures; he ascended into heaven and is seated at the right hand of the Father. He will come again in glory to judge the living and the dead, and his kingdom will have no end.

We believe in the Holy Spirit, the Lord, the giver of life, who proceeds from the Father and the Son. With the Father and the Son he is worshiped and glorified. He has spoken through the Prophets. We believe in one holy catholic [universal] and apostolic Church. We acknowledge one baptism for the forgiveness of sins. We look for the resurrection of the dead, and the life of the world to come. Amen.

Myths and Misconceptions

MYTH: Martin Luther left the Catholic Church to start a new church.

FACT: He was excommunicated by the Church against his will.

MYTH: Jonathan Edwards preached only hellfire-and-brimstone sermons.

FACT: Although he did preach so as to bring "the fear of God" into people, the majority of his sermons were positive, filled with promises and images of God's beauty.

MYTH: The Puritans were teetotalers.

FACT: They were known to drink plenty of beer and rum.

MYTH: All Puritan clergy were in favor of the Salem witch trials.

FACT: A number supported the trials. But some did not. The Puritan preachers Increase Mather and his son Cotton Mather insisted that wisdom and restraint prevail. They helped end the trials and did much to squelch the frenzy of that sad time.

MYTH: Harvard, Yale, and Princeton arose as intellectual centers to counter the effects of the Great Awakening.

FACT: Each of these "Ivies" originated as institutions for training evangelical ministers.

6

THE TWENTIETH CENTURY: THE ASSAULT ON BELIEF AND THE EVANGELICAL-FUNDAMENTALIST SPLIT

Evangelicalism did not "go the way of the dodo" in the twentieth century, as the late theologian and Trinity Seminary dean Kenneth Kantzer feared might happen. But it nearly did. The forces that shaped modern opposition to biblical beliefs were in part the outcome of an eighteenth-century German school of biblical scholarship called "higher criticism." Scholars of this school asserted that the authentic Jesus could not be fully known—the scriptures had been reworked by too many later writers who had tampered with and even made up events, including miracle narratives. In addition, advances in archaeology and the academic examination of Middle Eastern records caused some to look at early biblical documents in a new light. Prior to this, the assumption had been that biblical writings were divinely inspired and so unassailable. The attempts to validate the Bible through higher criticism and the scientific method became known in theological circles as "modernism," or "liberalism." It was based on the Enlightenment notion that only the mind could separate truth from error. Modernists asserted that religious teachings needed to adapt to rationalist terms. Other currents of thought that influenced modernism were Darwin's theory of evolution (*On the Origin of Species,*

1859), which challenged the historical veracity of the biblical account of creation; Freud's theories, which attributed human behavior to unconscious instincts and lower drives; Adam Smith's book *The Wealth of Nations* (1776), which advanced economics centered on self-interest: "The great affair, we always find, is to get money."

Modernism attacked the notions of justification by faith alone and *sola scriptura* put forth during the Reformation. If scripture was the authoritative guide to faith and practice, what was one to do with all these new and varying theories that challenged its precepts? The late Carl F. H. Henry said of this period: "Our century [the twentieth] has been one of the most turning and churning times in the history of humanity. Nowhere in the religious history of the West have the controlling beliefs of society changed so swiftly and as radically as in our twentieth-century struggle between theism and naturalism."

The term "fundamentalism" gained currency through a series of booklets published between 1910 and 1915, entitled "The Fundamentals: A Testimony to the Truth." These booklets were written by leading evangelical ministers and were distributed free to the clergy. Fundamentalism arose as a conservative response to the liberalizing influence of Darwin, Freud, and higher criticism. In 1920, a journalist and Baptist layman named Curtis Lee Laws adopted the term "fundamentalist" to denote those who were ready "to do battle royal for the Fundamentals." Between the 1920s and the early 1940s, evangelicalism and fundamentalism were considered more or less the same. They both upheld the "fundamentals," i.e., basic positive assertions that included the inspiration and authority of scripture; the deity of Jesus Christ; the virgin birth; the miracles, atoning death, physical resurrection, and eventual bodily return of Jesus; and human sin and salvation through spiritual regeneration. Such beliefs came increasingly under attack by modernist thinkers.

This conflict between evangelical and modernist ideologies came to an explosive climax in a muggy courtroom in Dayton, Tennessee, during the summer of 1925. The civil case was called *State v. John Scopes*—better known as "the Monkey Trial," the turning point in a downward trajectory for evangelical belief from which it has not fully recovered to this day.

In February of that year, Tennessee had enacted a bill making it unlawful "to teach any theory that denied the story of divine creation as taught by the Bible" and forbade the teaching that "man was descended from a lower order of animals." The defendant, John Scopes, a science teacher and football coach, had given an assignment to students from a textbook that introduced the theory of evolution. The lawyer for his defense, hired by the American Civil Liberties Union, was the arrogant and unabashed agnostic Clarence Darrow—*not* the ACLU's first choice. (They feared his agnosticism would antagonize the faith sensibilities of the jury.) But their first choice, science fiction writer H. G. Wells, had declined. The prosecution was headed by William Jennings Bryan, a renowned orator and three-time presidential candidate who had not, however, practiced law in thirty years.

In the end, Bryan prevailed; Darrow (and Scopes) lost. But it was a classic case of winning the battle while losing war. The carnival atmosphere surrounding the trial won no sympathy for Bible believers. Chimpanzees (said to be witnesses for the prosecution) performed sideshows while vendors at lemonade stands hawked T. T. Martin's books, *God—or Gorilla?* and *Hell and the High School*, claiming that teaching evolution would undermine the authority of the scriptures, sending readers down the path to atheism.

The two sides presented the contest as a cosmic battle between good and evil. Bryan said, "If evolution wins, Christianity goes." Darrow declared, "Scopes isn't on trial; civilization is on trial." On the seventh day of the trial, William Jennings Bryan was called to the stand to testify on his own behalf as a Bible expert. The *New York Times* called it "the most amazing court scene in Anglo-Saxon history."

Darrow peppered him with questions about biblical minutiae. Bryan rebuffed Darrow in exasperation, as noted in the followed snatches of dialogue:

> Darrow: Could you tell me how old the earth is?
> Bryan: No, sir, I couldn't.
> Darrow: Could you come anywhere near it?
> Bryan: I could possibly come as near as the scientists do, but I had rather be more accurate before I give a guess . . .
> D: Do you believe the first woman was Eve?
> B: Yes.
> D: Do you believe she was literally made out of Adam's rib?
> B: I do.
> D: Did you ever discover where Cain got his wife?
> B: No, sir, I leave the agnostics to hunt for her.

During the interrogation one of the prosecuting attorneys objected, asking the purpose of this line of inquiry. Bryan jumped in: "I am perfectly willing that the world shall know that these gentlemen have no other purpose than ridiculing every Christian who believes in the Bible," to which Darrow responded, "We have the purpose of preventing bigots and ignoramuses from controlling the education of the United States."

Bryan answered, "I am simply trying to protect the Word of God against the greatest atheist or agnostic in the United States."

As Darrow's interrogation continued, focusing on the date of the Flood, the exasperated Bryan said, "I've never made the calculation." Darrow asked, "What do you think?" Bryan answered, "I do not think about things I don't think about." Darrow seized the opportunity to make his antagonist look the fool: "Do you think about the things you do think about?"

One paper described the ill and aging Bryan as "a punch-drunk warrior." The *Christian Century* called Darrow "an embarrassment and misfortune."

Darrow himself requested a guilty verdict so he could appeal the case at the Tennessee Supreme Court. The jury complied. The judge fined the defense one hundred dollars. Six days later, William Jennings Bryan died in his sleep. A year later, the Tennessee Supreme Court reversed the Dayton court's decision on a technicality (the fine should have been set by the jury, not the judge) and dismissed the case, noting, "Nothing is to be gained by prolonging the life of this bizarre case."

EVANGELICAL RESPONSE TO THE MONKEY TRIAL

The Scopes trial precipitated a crisis for evangelicals, who were then known as fundamentalists. Fundamentalism had taken on a social stigma as a result of the trial. That left those who upheld biblical "fundamentals" looking like unintellectual court jesters. The caricature had grown so widespread that social commentator H. L. Mencken (who'd covered the trial) said at the time, "Heave an egg out a Pullman window, and you will hit a fundamentalist anywhere in the United States." Even so, when it came to social influence, liberalism had permeated mainline denominations, such as Baptists and Presbyterians, and wielded a strong influence on culture. In a circuitous way, however, the crisis rallied the fundamentalists to reassert the trustworthiness of the Bible, the role of the supernatural, and the operations of the Holy Spirit in a believer's life. This, in turn, created a dividing line between those who identified themselves as evangelicals, and those who held a defensive position in the fundamentalist camp. (More on this split follows.)

Two additional streams of Bible-based Christian belief closely associated with fundamentalism asserted themselves during this period: dispensationalism and Pentecostalism. Each in its own way manifested (if unintentionally) a response to certain aspects of modernism that had threatened belief.

Dispensationalism, discussed in chapter 4, divided time into epochs of God's saving activity. The "great parentheses," as John Nelson Darby called the epoch of the present age (during which God's activities were less overt), imposed a divine order that overruled the random chaos of natural selection as the means of forward movement.

Pentecostalism also flourished during this time. An outgrowth of its antecedent, the Holiness movement, Pentecostalism derived its name from Acts 2, in which the Holy Spirit descended on the gathered believers like "tongues of fire" and gave them the gift of understanding one another's languages, as well as the supernatural power to heal and perform miracles. Pentecostals' intuitive, experienced-based expression of faith emphasized the role of the Holy Spirit in conferring extraordinary gifts to the people of God, male and female. These gifts often included glossolalia (speaking in tongues, or unintelligible prayer language), miracles of healing, and a victorious claim on God's power. Other gifts included the ability to teach and prophesy, to discern spirits, cast out demons, and give to the poor. One's station in life, as well as one's gender, were irrelevant. The Spirit gifted and empowered those he willed with whatever gifts the Spirit desired. Therefore, leadership roles in the church were granted not on the basis of academic credentials, but on the Spirit's gifting. Pentecostalism, with its emphasis on supernatural empowerment of believers, challenged Freud's notion that humans were driven by subconscious forces. It also overturned the presuppositions of naturalism that only what is visible is real.

AIMEE SEMPLE MCPHERSON

As I ponder and pray in the stillness, I dream as a dreamer of dreams. A steepled church stands before me—a church with open doors. Within it I see the preacher stand; hear his voice in earnest call. But 'tis the throng that flows through the street outside that hold my anxious gaze. . . . "And we," say the heavy, groping, lonely feet, "are bereaved and seek comfort and rest. For us the shades of night are falling. The knowledge that Christ 'once' dried tears and bore the heavy load is blest indeed, but Oh! we of today need succor now. Preaching "The Great I Was" can never satisfy our longings. We need "The Great I Am."

(From her sermon "The Great 'I Am' or 'I Was' ")

Pentecostalism was born during the Azusa Street revival led by African-American preacher William Seymour in a run-down mission in Los Angeles early in 1906. It gained new adherents during 1920s under the ministry of Aimee Semple McPherson. Her teachings focused on a "four square" approach to the gospel: "Jesus, the Only Savior; Jesus, the Great Physician; Jesus, the Baptizer with the Holy Spirit; Jesus the Coming Bridegroom, Lord and King." Her ministry included outreach to prostitutes, the homeless, and the infirm, inviting them to be restored to health and wholeness. The denomination she founded remains two million strong to this day—the International Church of the Foursquare Gospel.

Pentecostalism (likened to today's "charismatic") remains robust today. It is the fastest-growing Christian movement in Latin America and fills churches in South Korea with six-figure member counts. Like evangelicalism, it is like a stream that flows into many diverse denominations, including the Catholic, Episcopalian, and Lutheran churches, as well as non-denominational storefronts.

The modernist period extended from about 1900 to 1940, when 25 percent of churches in the U.S. were dominated by liberalism. By around 1930 conservative Protestantism reached its lowest ebb. However, it continued to flourish among people who emphasized the mystery of God's activity (dispensationalists) and the supernatural operations of the Spirit (Pentecostalism). These movements kept the fires burning, but they also bequeathed to evangelicalism a legacy of anti-intellectualism.

At the time, fundamentalists viewed with suspicion the way in which the scriptures were studied at seminaries. Rather than engage in scriptural criticism, they looked to the Spirit for "a word from the Lord." They retreated from intellectual involvement

─────────────────────── How Come? ───────────────────────

What Do Evangelicals Believe About Evolution?

Theories of creation can be a source of heated debate within evangelical circles, as they are in the world at large. Some, who call themselves "six-day creationists," believe that when the Book of Genesis says God created the heavens and the earth in seven days (six days of creation, the seventh a day of rest), it refers to a twenty-four-hour day. This would put the earth's age in the vicinity of six-thousand-plus years. This introduces complications into how to interpret the fossil record, which posits the beginning of life on earth at four billion years ago. The word for "day" used in the original language of the Old Testament—Hebrew—is *yom* (as in the Jewish holy day *Yom Kippur*—Day of Atonement). But *yom*, as it is used in the Old Testament, also occurs in a variety of contexts besides a literal twenty-four-hour day. For example, it is used to describe "the day of the Lord" (2 Peter says, "One day with the Lord is as a thousand years"; and Psalm 90 notes, "For a thousand years in Your sight are like a day that has just gone by"), which carries cosmic implications beyond time and place. Thus other evangelicals demur from six-day creationism and do not fear the fossil record. They allow for the possibility that God may have used an evolutionary process to unfold his creative masterpiece. For the most part, though, evangelicals deny evolution as a theory of *creation* and rally around "intelligent design" (ID), asserting that the universe was designed by a superior intelligence (God) and was not the result of random chance. Evidence in favor of ID includes the exceptional fine-tuning of certain physical constants of the universe, as well as certain biological phenomena (such as the human eye or the body's blood clotting mechanisms) that seem to be "irreducibly complex." ID proponents maintain that this complexity is sufficiently great that a pathway of mutations and natural selection couldn't get you from point A to point B. This theory has also captured the interest of some nonevangelical scientists. (See *Darwin's Black Box* in the Suggested Reading section at the back of the book.)

---

with a changing world and rejected the possibility of deriving any instruction from it. The enduring impact of this period was the loss of evangelical institutions of higher learning, from which evangelicalism is only now beginning to recover. Universities and academies such as Harvard, Yale, Union, and Andover, originally beacons of evangelical intellectualism, dropped their allegiance to it and even became hostile toward this kind of faith. Mark Noll, the McManis Professor of Christian Thought at Wheaton College, says that the era of modernism "was a drastic time that required drastic remedies. Although I think the remedies were extreme and ended up in unwise excesses, they were basically good. I have one qualification, however: our institutions were not only taken away. I think, in part, they were given away." He means that the fundamentalist retreat from the world generally, and the academy specifically, left a vacuum filled by modernist antagonists.

The unwelcoming environment in the academy, in turn, brought about two shifts within the movement itself: a marked split between evangelicals and fundamentalists, and a defensive and at times simplistic approach to what became known as the Battle for the Bible.

THE EVANGELICAL-FUNDAMENTALIST SPLIT

In the early 1940s, a distinct split grew between evangelicals and fundamentalists over how to apply the fundamentals of faith to the modern world. In 1941 the Reverend Carl McIntire founded the American Council of Christian Churches, an extremist group that favored separatism from hostile cultural forces. Some went so far as to refuse contact with anyone who *did* interact with the larger culture. Not all fundamentalists felt this way, however. One branch of Bible believers—evangelicals—wanted to engage the culture, while the other branch—fundamentalists—moved away from it, sometimes belligerently. Kenneth Kantzer, a keen observer of the changing picture, said that for many evangelicals who had considered themselves fundamentalists, the term became "an embarrassment instead of a badge of honor."

At the time, evangelicals did not see themselves as rebelling against fundamentalism. Rather, they saw themselves as sincere believers who longed for a "Bible-believing" pastor with an education—one who could approach contemporary issues with intellect and eloquence. Scholars like Kantzer, Harold Ockenga, and Carl F. H. Henry did not, of necessity, reject every idea set forth by modernists simply because they were modern. They did not fear cultural involvement or conflicting viewpoints; they were deeply committed to social action and justice.

A number of institutions and organizations became rallying points under the flag of evangelicalism. In 1942, Harold Ockenga spearheaded the formation of the National Association of Evangelicals (NAE) as a platform for conservative Christians who wanted to be culturally engaged. Carl Henry wrote *The Uneasy Conscience of Modern Fundamentalism* (1947), which offered a strong critique of fundamentalist separatism, charging a betrayal of their own heritage. The same year saw the formation of one of evangelicalism's hallmark seminaries, Fuller Theological Seminary in Pasadena, California. Two years later Billy Graham gained national headlines at his Los Angeles tent meetings when newspaper magnate William Randolph Hearst told his editors to "puff Graham," catapulting him onto the national stage. This made "crusade evangelism" front-page news. In 1950 Billy Graham and Harold Ockenga both spoke in the Rose Bowl, addressing the largest audience ever at any religious gathering in the Pacific Southwest. By 1956 Graham had launched *Christianity Today,* a new magazine "of evangelical conviction." All of this signaled a new day.

Evangelicals took on what Carl Henry called "the costly burden of creating evangelical scholarship in a world that's in rebellion." He meant that as the effects of the Enlightenment permeated the culture, God seemed to have become irrelevant. Evangelicals assumed the responsibility of making God relevant again, and in a way that was accessible to the culture at large.

THE INERRANCY OF THE BIBLE

The word *inerrancy* is derived from the Latin, meaning "not wandering." Its usage in this context implies "not wandering from the truth." For evangelicals, inerrancy means that when scripture says something, it is telling the truth and not "wandering" into falsehood. Does this mean that evangelicals believe God dictated the Bible word for word, thus making each word unflawed? Many would say no. But if you asked if they embraced the traditional tenets of faith of the Protestant Reformation—the authority of the scripture, the virgin birth and divinity of Christ, Jesus' atonement for sin, the bodily resurrection, and the second coming of Christ—evangelicals would say yes, unequivocally.

InterVarsity Christian Fellowship, a student-led college ministry originating in England (1877) but established in the United States in 1941, includes in its statement of faith a definition of inerrancy that most evangelicals find helpful: "the unique divine inspiration, entire trustworthiness and authority of the Bible." Evangelicals believe that scripture gives truth—and not only truth, but divine authority for belief and behavior. For example, Jesus tells his followers not to return evil for evil. Therefore, if an evangelical is maligned by someone else, he or she is obligated not to escalate hostilities by responding in kind. (They don't always succeed, but the scripture gives them a principle to aspire to.) To give another example, the book of James says, "Confess your sins to each other and pray for each other so you can be healed" (5:16). This compels evangelicals to confess their failures to one another. (Here again, it doesn't always play out this way, but it gives an ideal of behavior.)

THE BATTLE FOR THE BIBLE

The Battle for the Bible, as it came to be called, was the attempt by evangelicals to take on the higher critics and modernists on the issue of scriptural integrity. The contest between liberals and evangelicals was not a barroom brawl but a sparring through academic conferences, papers, confessions, statements, books, and other paths of biblical scholarship over a forty-year period, from the 1940s to the 1980s. For example, the founding statement of the Evangelical Theological Society (1949) reads: "The Bible alone, and the Bible in its entirety, is the Word of God, written, and therefore inerrant in the autographs" (autographs are the written originals, presumably reflected in existing manuscripts). Almost thirty years later, in 1978, the Chicago Statement of Biblical Inerrancy declared: "Inerrant signifies the quality of being free from all falsehood or mistake and so safeguards the truth that Holy Scripture is entirely true and trustworthy in all its assertions" (*assertions*— not every jot and tittle).

The evangelical aim in the Battle for the Bible was to reclaim scripture from the modernist interpretation that it was unreliable. For example, modernists said that the Bible "contained" elements that could be considered a word from God; evangelicals countered that the Bible in its entirety *is* the Word of God. Modernists said the death of Jesus was a heroic model of self-denying love; evangelicals asserted it was far more than an example: it was a cosmic realignment through which the sacrifice of Jesus restored the wreckage manifested at the Fall. Modernists said humanity could be saved only through good works of charity and social redemption; evangelicals responded (following Luther) that as important as those works might be, humanity could be saved only through faith in Jesus, from which good works then emanate.

Evangelical scholars argued that, despite liberals' noble intentions of validating scripture for a modernist world, they did so at the expense of the very faith they were trying to preserve. A leader in criticizing the modernist approach to Bible scholarship was a British Anglican evangelical named James Innell (J. I.) Packer. Billy Graham had taken his crusade across the Atlantic in 1954–55 and aroused an enthusiasm that unsettled the Anglican establishment. Then Canon H. K. Luce published an article asking "Is it not time that our religious leaders made it plain that while they respect, or even admire, Dr. Graham's sincerity and personal power, they cannot regard fundamentalism [here Luce means evangelicalism] as like to issue in anything but disillusionment and disaster for educated men and women in this 20th century?"

J. I. Packer answered this question, offering what his biographer Alister McGrath calls "the definitive evangelical response." In his book *Fundamentalism and the Word of God* (1958) Packer demonstrated that evangelical assumptions about the Bible carried a logic and intellectual rigor that modernist theologians had abdicated in their liberal approach. He asserted, "The truth is that Liberalism was a deduction from the 19th-century view of 'religion' . . . with the characteristic 19th-century scientific outlook." That being the case, he argued, liberal "scholarship" did not allow biblical scholarship to be undertaken on its own terms, but only through what modernism presupposed could be seen—which meant that nothing could be seen that would contradict the realm of reason. The result, Packer told me, was to show that "the criticisms . . . applied to the critics much more than they applied to those at whom they were first directed [evangelicals]." Packer's book, wrote the (British) *Evangelical Times,* "lifted the drooping head" of an entire generation. He challenged modernist skeptics on the grounds of sheer logic and showed, using the same logic, that the scriptures could be trusted.

In retrospect, some evangelicals have wondered how beneficial the Battle for the Bible has been in the development of evangelical thought. Was it only about distrust of the liberal academy and, in reaction, a defensive, isolated form of Biblical scholarship? Fuller Theological Seminary president Richard Mouw says that the inerrancy debate helped "spell out what we mean by the Word." He added, "It has also guarded the message that Scripture is precious." Nevertheless, most scholars agree that it is not so much biblical inerrancy that lies at the core of evangelical faith. The larger issue, as articulated by Kenneth Kantzer, is "the person of Jesus Christ, and what to do with him."

J. I. PACKER

We should not abandon faith in anything that God has taught us merely because we cannot solve all the problems which it raises. Our own intellectual competence is not the test and measure of divine truth. It is not for us to stop believing because we lack understanding, or to postpone believing till we can get understanding, but to believe in order that we may understand. This is the core issue of authority—are we going to trust our own minds, or are we going to trust God's Word?

(Fundamentalism and the Word of God)

Trivia Quiz

1) Who said, "Here I stand, I can do no other?"

A) Billy Graham to Khrushchev

B) Jimmy Swaggart to his congregation while confessing sexual sin

C) Martin Luther during his heresy trial before Catholic authorities

D) Arnold Schwarzenegger in *Terminator 2*

[Answer: C]

2) The acronym TULIP helps us remember the five points of Calvinism. What do the letters stand for?

A) Ten Ugly Lousy Itinerant Preachers

B) Teach Us Love, Intimacy, Peace

C) Teachers United Loudly to Intimidate Parents

D) Total depravity, Unconditional election, Limited atonement, Irresistible grace, Perseverance of the saints

[Answer: D]

3) Shine, Jesus, Shine is:

A) Furniture polish available only in Family Christian Stores

B) A favorite praise chorus

C) What Paul said to Jesus during his vision on the road to Damascus

D) The visual effect of Grandma's painting of Jesus on black velvet

[Answer: B]

4) Who said, "Could Jesus microwave a burrito so hot that even he couldn't eat it?"

A) Rudolph Bultmann

B) Albert Einstein

C) Enrique Iglesias

D) Homer Simpson

[Answer: D]

5) Which well-loved hymns were written by Charles Wesley, brother of the more famous preacher John Wesley, founder of Methodism?

A) Hark! The Herald Angels Sing

B) A Charge to Keep I Have

C) Christ the Lord Is Risen Today

D) Jesus, Lover of My Soul

E) All of the above

[Answer: E]

7

EVANGELICALS AND CULTURE

Modernism and its related isms were not the only cultural forces that positioned twentieth-century evangelicalism as a populist movement. America's post–World War II wealth similarly transformed its social dynamics, which in turn left their mark on the way people "did church."

Prior to the Great Depression and World War II, the concept of "youth culture" did not exist. It arose with the industrial age, and the subsequent period of prosperity. Young people, born in the years after the war, crashed onto the scene in huge numbers. Inevitably, groups sprang up to entertain and educate them—including Christian organizations such as Young Life and Youth for Christ. As a result, "youth ministry" was born.

Leisure, prosperity, and sheer numbers made the baby boomer generation a force to be reckoned with as they rewrote the rules of American culture. They grew disaffected with "the establishment" and eschewed institutionalized anything, including church.

That disaffection, in turn, produced yet another turn of the cultural wheel: the "Jesus People" movement. Though the Jesus People movement started in various places around the country as part of the counterculture of the time, most scholars point to its real beginning as the 1967 opening of the Living Room in southern California. Here, young Christians reached out with their message of the Gospel to other countercultural hippies—and converted thousands. These animated young Christians came from Haight-Ashbury (San Francisco's hotbed of hippiedom); "Surf City," California; small towns in Ohio; and New York's Hell's Kitchen.

This movement coalesced the free-floating radical and creative zeitgeist with unprecedented evangelical fervor. While many in their generation were getting high on drugs, this idealistic cohort was "high on Jesus."

EVANGELICAL POPULISM

Other youth ministries also gained huge numbers of members at this time. In addition to the InterVarsity Christian Fellowship, mentioned earlier, groups like the Navigators (originally started for sailors in the 1930s), Young Life, and others made significant inroads in reaching baby boomers with an evangelical Christian message.

Perhaps the most influential mover and shaker behind the Christian youth movement was Bill Bright, who in 1951, with his wife Vonette, founded Campus Crusade for Christ. Bright and his organization came up with an idea that ultimately mobilized tens of thousands of young Jesus freaks and helped change the face of American evangelicalism. An astute businessman, Bright realized the best way to attract his potential market was to refine and package the Gospel message. So he created a handy yellow tract that fit into a shirt pocket or a wallet, summarizing what he called the "Four Spiritual Laws":

- God loves you and offers a wonderful plan for your life.
- Humans are sinful and separated from God, and thus cannot know and experience God's love and plan.
- Jesus Christ is God's only provision for humanity's sin.
- We must individually receive Jesus as Savior and Lord.

Years later J. I. Packer remarked, "Some brilliant people are able to come up with a formula to fit almost everybody. Henry Ford did it with the Model T; Bill Bright did it with the Four Spiritual Laws." Bright, who died in 2003, gave his organization a single goal: to reach "every human on earth" with the Christian gospel.

Newsweek declared 1976 the "Year of the Evangelical," as Campus Crusade along with the other youth organizations rose in popularity. Jimmy Carter, outspoken in his identity as an evangelical, was elected president. A year later, in 1977, Charles Colson's book *Born Again* sold a half million copies, and televangelist Pat Robertson opened CBN University (for Christian Broadcasting Network), later renamed Regent University. By 1978, "Jesus festivals" featuring a new kind of music called Christian rock drew tens of thousands of teens. This energized youth movement spurred the growth of the contemporary Christian music industry and other Christian entertainment media.

In 1979, a Gallup poll showed that the number of evangelicals in the United States had grown from 40 million to 70 million in thirty years. And by 1980 they had turned into an influential voting bloc that helped get Ronald Reagan elected to the White House.

Evangelical culture was making its way into the mainstream as well. Amy Grant paved the way for Christian contemporary music (as it has come to be called) to find an audience on non-Christian radio. Soon innovators and edgier versions of "Christian music" groups would follow, like dcTalk and Jars of Clay. Later decades would witness the rise of organizations like the Fellowship of Christian Athletes, Christian kids' videos (Veggie Tales), and even kitschy "Christian" art, like Thomas Kinkade's sentimental landscapes and thatched-roof country cottages.

CONFRONTING CULTURE

By the mid-1970s evangelicals were no longer an embattled minority. Their social advances emboldened them to go out and engage the culture. And they did so—energetically. The populist evangelicalism that arose from this period, however, has since been criticized as angry and rigid in tone, lacking in humility and self-examination. Mark Noll wrote in his book *The Scandal of the Evangelical Mind* that "popular authority figures" contributed to an intellectual environment in evangelicalism that was "naive, inept, or tendentious." This was most vividly evidenced in two social issues that have been confronting American culture since that time—abortion and gay rights.

A gay friend of mine asked me recently, "Why is it that gays and abortion are at the top of the evangelical agenda? How did homosexuality leap over murder and adultery?" My friend is correct when he asserts that these cultural trends triggered an especially heated response from evangelicals, although they are hardly monolithic in how they address these issues. Even if not all evangelicals agree on homosexuality and abortion, they all look to scripture to figure out what they should believe. The evangelical take on these topics, in part, is rooted in the first chapter of Genesis: At creation, God created man and woman in his image and told them to have dominion over the earth and multiply. According to the Bible, then, God established humanity as made in God's image with the family as the centerpiece and heterosexual relationships as the God-given model. When abortion and gay rights entered the cultural conversation, they challenged what evangelicals believe is God's intention for humanity in both of these realms.

The conflict between evangelicals and pro-choice and gay rights activists has been hostile. A defining year, and one that set the tone for subsequent antagonism, was 1989. That year, the gay-activist group ACT-UP (AIDS Coalition To Unleash Power) disrupted a worship service at St. Patrick's Cathedral in New York City, chaining themselves to the pews and desecrating the Eucharist by spitting the wafers on the floor (though some evangelicals don't believe the consecrated host is the body of Christ, they were shocked at the sacrilege). The same year, Randall Terry founded Operation Rescue, a pro-life protest organization that staged sit-ins to rally evangelicals at abortion clinics. Pro-choice advocates saw Operation Rescue as an assault on the freedom of women who were trying to get a legal abortion. The situation worsened when, in some cases, violent incidents occurred outside the clinics—tactics the majority of evangelicals publicly condemned. In each case, a few extremist acts escalated hostilities between both sides and put them on the defensive. The actions of fringe groups distorted the picture of the whole, and as a result, each side stubbornly refused to give ground.

IMAGE PROBLEMS

The anger generated over abortion and gay rights became a kind of "marketing problem" for evangelicals. Instead of responding to gay rights activists in a measured, cogent, and circumspect way, they came across as judgmental and self-righteous. On abortion rights, they were on firm theological ground—but the majority of Americans continued to profess pro-choice views, which the courts and the laws upheld. As a result, hope for honest engagement on both fronts was lost.

What has caused evangelicals to be seen in such an unsympathetic light? Explains Fuller Theological School president Richard Mouw, "In the political sphere, we went from unthinking noninvolvement to unthinking involvement, which translated into the triumphalistic takeover mentality not guided by careful theological reflection."

Evangelicals entered the public square with religious conviction and guided by the authority of the Bible, which (more or less) united them on certain issues. But they have been criticized for the selective use of Bible passages, especially in addressing the gay rights issue.

The Apostle Paul writes about sin in the New Testament. Some sins at first glance seem much worse than others, such as murder or the slave trade (1 Timothy 1:10). Others seem more innocuous: thievery, greed, drunkenness, abuse, swindling (1 Corinthians 6:9); anger, rage, malicious behavior, slander, bad language (Colossians 3:8); hate, envy, fighting, backstabbing, insolence, pride, heartlessness, ruthlessness, lack of forgiveness, and boastfulness (Romans 1:29–30). Nevertheless, Paul includes homosexuality in both categories: "Those who indulge in sexual sin, . . . male prostitutes [and] homosexuals . . . will have no share in the Kingdom of God" (1 Corinthians 6:9).

Elsewhere he says, "Women turned against the natural way to have sex and instead indulged in sex with each other. And men, instead of having normal sex relationships with women, burned with lust for each other. Men did shameful things with other men and, as a result, suffered within themselves" (Romans 1:26–27). The point is, for Paul, the seemingly really bad sins as well as innocuous ones carry the same result: alienation from God.

But evangelicals have tended to isolate homosexuality as a more virulent strain of human rebellion than the other forms of sin, such as materialism, gossip, and gluttony. Yet these "sins"—reckoning the term in its classical theological sense—carry as much weight as homosexuality. Evangelicals have put homosexuality in a category all its own while whitewashing pathologies rampant in their own community. This has made them look like hypocrites and has inflicted pain and heartache on the gay community.

When it comes to abortion, many Christian ethicists believe that evangelicals have more theological ground on which to stand. The Bible clearly states in the Ten Commandments that murder is wrong. And many people, including those who are pro-choice, believe that human life begins at least in some form at conception. Therefore, evangelicals see abortion as a human rights issue. But evangelicals' appeal to logic did not work to advance the debate. Nor has their appeal to divine prerogatives condemning murder. In 1996 Michael Kinsley wrote in *Time* magazine, "The battle over abortion is over, and the prochoicers have won."

Evangelicals do not concede that it is over, however. They have in fact likened it to the slavery issue that led to the Civil War. Senator Sam Brownback, an evangelical Republican from

Kansas, compared abortion (and human cloning) to chattel slavery. "The basic question," he said, "is whether the young human is a person or property . . . livestock, to be treated as its master chooses."

Even so, those in the forefront of the pro-life movement would like to see engagement move to higher ground.

WHAT WOULD JESUS DO?

No evangelical can get away from the words of Jesus, who said, "Love your enemies and pray for those who persecute you." Most, if they were honest and had the chance, would pull Jesus aside and say, "What were you *thinking*?" Loving one's enemies is not natural. But for Christians, that is exactly the point. They'd have to say, to be theologically consistent, that Jesus would answer the question this way: "Well, what I was thinking when I said 'Love your enemies' was that doing so exhibits the qualities of God, who loves you. And you, after all, have shown yourself to be his enemy."

I'm not suggesting that gay activists and pro-choice advocates are looked upon as the enemy by evangelicals. The larger point is, Jesus' command to love your enemies should have moved the debate to a different level, at least for evangelicals.

Evangelicals' alienation from gay activists and pro-choice advocates is partly a result of the tribalism that marks our age. But tribalism alone doesn't account for the hostilities between the camps. It comes down to one's source of authority—and each group turns to a different authority for moral choices. My gay friend, for example, says he happens to think the Apostle Paul is wrong in what he says about homosexuality. He believes that God made gay people as they are for a reason, regardless of what Paul says. But evangelicals trust the authority of Paul's words, even if they don't understand or even agree. All three groups base their convictions on belief: For gays, it is belief in their right to be who they are; for pro-choice advocates, it is belief in a woman's right to choose; for evangelicals, it is belief that abortion is murder and homosexuality outside God's design, and that it is their right to express their conviction (regardless of current legalities—given that slavery was also once legal). The debate cannot move forward if any party demands that the others abdicate conscience before dialogue can ensue. But all must concede that conviction by itself does not forfeit honest debate. Evangelicals have been misunderstood as coming from a place of bigotry and hate rather than from a place of conviction and conscience. Perhaps at times they have expressed themselves badly, but many regret past mistakes and would like to start a new conversation.

----------------- How Come? -----------------

Do Evangelicals Regard Jerry Falwell and Pat Robertson as Their Spokespersons?

Reverend Jerry Falwell rose to prominence in the 1980s as one of the founders of the Moral Majority. Today he is president of Liberty University and pastor of the Thomas Road Baptist Church in Lynchburg, Virginia. Pat Robertson is a religious broadcaster, businessman, and founder of the Christian Broadcasting Network (CBN), International Family Entertainment, Inc., and Regent University. Both men are prominent and controversial media personalities who tend to dominate public perceptions of evangelicals' views. But do all evangelicals share their opinions?

It depends. Evangelicals inclined toward conservative political activism embrace their call to get involved. Robertson, who is a Charismatic, adds the element of summoning the supernatural intervention of the Holy Spirit to turn events (more so than Falwell, who is Southern Baptist). He was ridiculed in 1993 when he prayed on his television program *The 700 Club* for "a wall of protection" from Hurricane Isabel to surround Virginia Beach.

Less politically oriented evangelicals, or those whose politics are left-leaning, cringe at the swagger of both men and become embarrassed by less-than-thoughtful public statements. For example, after the September 11 tragedy, Falwell said (on Robertson's *700 Club*): "I really believe that the pagans, and the abortionists, and the feminists, and the gays and the lesbians who are actively trying to make that an alternative lifestyle, the ACLU, People For the American Way, all of them who have tried to secularize America. I point the finger in their face and say 'you helped this happen.' " The National Gay and Lesbian Task Force demanded an apology from Falwell, who did amend his statement on CNN: "I would never blame any human being except the terrorists, and if I left that impression with gays or lesbians or anyone else, I apologize."

8

Politics Past, Present, and Future

America has from the beginning been a nation bent on redemption. That, after all, is what John Winthrop was getting at in 1630 when he famously predicted, "We shall be a city upon a hill." The struggle to define what needs saving by whom has been fought out continually on a variety of battlefields. And it continues today, in what Nobel laureate Robert Foel recently called our "Fourth Great Awakening": a new religious revival fueled by revulsion with the corruptions of a contemporary society.

—MICHAEL KAZIN, "THE POLITICS OF DEVOTION" IN *THE NATION*
(APRIL 6, 1998)

The embattled position in which evangelicals found themselves in the late twentieth century inevitably led to their elbowing their way to a place at the political table. It could be argued that evangelicals did not move into politics so much as politics moved into their domain: faith and morality. Evangelicals believed the courts were blithely translating into law notions that arose from the 1960s cultural revolution—with *Roe v. Wade* as a case in point. As a result, many felt compelled to get involved.

The defining year that set the terms for evangelicals' cultural engagement over abortion and gay rights was 1989, as mentioned earlier. It was also the year that evangelicals effectively mobilized a political machine—the Christian Coalition, founded by Christian broadcaster Pat Robertson after his unsuccessful bid for the Republican presidential nomination in 1988. The goal of the Christian Coalition was the election of Christian conservatives to important public offices through a network of statewide organizations. Previously, in the late 1970s, the Reverend Jerry Falwell (and others) had launched his Moral Majority campaign; Dr. James Dobson, founder of Focus on the Family, picked up the theme in the early 1980s by placing abortion at the top of his list of threats to the family, and thus to society. By the time the Christian Coalition came along, evangelicals were ripe to meet these issues head on. The group's first rally in Orlando in 1989 drew only six hundred supporters. But six years later, in the mid-1990s, under the savvy and intuitive leadership of executive director Ralph Reed, the Christian Coalition claimed membership of around 1.6 million, with two thousand local chapters. Though these numbers have been disputed, the Christian Coalition helped usher in the "Republican revolution" of 1994, the Newt Gingrich–led Republican Party's takeover of Congress, causing *Time* to hail Reed as the "right hand of God."

Reed wrote in his book *Active Faith* that the Christian Coalition was "a middle-class, highly educated suburban phenomenon of baby boomers with children who are motivated by their concerns about the family." (He may have been backhandedly countering the *Washington Post*'s widely criticized 1993 caricature of evangelicals as "largely poor, uneducated and easy to command.")

But membership plummeted after Bob Dole's failed presidential run in 1996 and Reed's subsequent resignation as Christian Coalition president in 1997. Then, in 1999, the IRS denied the organization tax-exempt status because of its political activism. For years it reeled from these losses, though according to coalition spokesman Drew McKissick, the organization has had an upsurge in membership because of issues such as terrorism and gay marriage (in the summer of 2004, McKissick noted, the coalition was emphasizing "voter identification, voter registration, and voter education"). Ralph Reed, now a private political consultant, was hired by the Republican Party as chairman of President Bush's 2004 Southeastern United States reelection campaign.

The Christian Coalition gave the false impression that evangelicals were a monolithic, right-wing political force that intended to foist religion on everybody, come hell or high water. Although some 83 percent of evangelicals identify themselves as conservative Republicans, a significant minority lean more to the left on social issues like poverty and the environment, and on foreign policy. In 1995, Jim Wallis, editor of the progressive Christian magazine *Sojourners*, started a Christian poverty activism group named Call to Renewal, as an alternative to the Christian Coalition. One prominent supporter was outspoken sociology professor and evangelical Baptist minister Tony Campolo, who diverges from the right-wing stereotype of evangelical political activism. In an August 2004 interview with Beliefnet, Campolo said, "When I read the voter guide of a group like the Christian Coalition, I find that they are allied with the National Rifle Association and are very anxious to protect the rights of people to buy even assault weapons. But they don't seem to be very supportive of concerns for the poor, concerns for trade relations, for canceling Third World debts. In short, there's a whole group of issues [including the environment] that are being ignored by the Religious Right and that warrant the attention of Bible-believing Christians."

In a forum on evangelicals and politics sponsored by *Christianity Today*, Ralph Reed denied attempting to turn religion into legislation. "My call for political involvement is based upon a biblical doctrine of citizenship that we should be 'salt and light,' a call to civic engagement in a fallen world. But to attempt to take theological precepts, even broadly defined, and legislate them on people who do not share those is a recipe for disaster. It's not only bad politics, it's bad theology." However, Reed also asserted that Christians must become involved in politics as a means of introducing moral constraints on the wider society, citing Martin Luther King, Jr.: "I cannot pass a law that will force the white man to love me, but I can pass a law to stop him from lynching me."

To Charles Colson, the career of William Wilberforce is a model for evangelical activism in politics. It was Wilberforce's faith that drove his forty-year commitment to abolishing slavery. "To me, abortion is a moral equivalent of slavery," Colson said in the same *CT* forum. "And so Christians belong in there with a Christian banner flying." Colson argued that all legislation is morally based, which means it has moral implications and affects moral behavior. He was careful, however, to render a caveat about the limits of politics: "My worry about the Christian Coalition or the Call to Renewal or any other group that is organized as a Christian political movement is that we're redressing [issues] through political means, which to me is a very limited remedy." The profound cultural transformation can take place, he said, "only when people ask themselves 'How shall we live?' "

Over the decades leading up to the new millennium, the evangelical movement saw many and varied peaks and valleys. By 1985, mainline denominational churches were losing members while evangelical churches were booming. The "megachurch"—auditoriums filled with thousands of believers—emerged as a paradigm in the Church Growth movement, a notion spurred in the 1970s and '80s by C. Peter Wagner during his twenty-eight-year tenure as Professor of Church Growth at Fuller Theological Seminary School of World Missions. His thesis that people worshiped more naturally in "homogeneous units" and in a non-threatening context evolved into the "seeker-sensitive movement," embodied most notably in Willow Creek Community Church (Barrington, Illinois) and its founder, Pastor Bill Hybels. This approach removed the trappings of "church" and made Sunday mornings an orchestrated, upbeat stage event in order to attract seekers who felt funny in church. (Services for mature worshipers would take place on a midweek night.) During this time, popular evangelical singer Amy Grant released her *Unguarded* album, blazing the trail for Christian artists to cross over into the mainstream.

Still, it was not all smooth sailing as far as public perception of the evangelical community. In 1987 Jim Bakker's PTL (Praise the Lord) media empire imploded because of financial and sexual scandals. Oral Roberts announced God would "take him home" if he didn't get $8 million for his hospital. Pat Robertson declared a bold but failed run for the White House. A year later, televangelist Jimmy Swaggart confessed to "personal sins" in an attempt to save his television ministry. He refused to step down and accept church discipline—so his denomination, the Assemblies of God, gave him the boot.

In the 1990 presidential election, evangelicals flexed political muscle, helping mainline Episcopalian George H. W. Bush win the White House. (Eighty-two percent of evangelicals voted for Bush.) Four years later Bill Clinton, a Southern Baptist who attended his wife's Methodist church, bounced him out. But Clinton's pro-choice position on abortion as well as his stance on other social issues, and his questionable personal morality, offended many evangelicals. Despite their clamor, he won again in 1996, deflating some evangelicals' confidence in political means of bringing moral reform to the country.

On other fronts, the evangelical movement got a shot of testosterone through the men's movement called Promise Keepers, founded by former football coach Bill McCartney. Emerging in 1993 when more than fifty thousand men gathered at the University of Colorado stadium for a rally, guys in ball caps and some with beer bellies celebrated manhood and fatherhood and vowed to honor wives and work harder to lead families. The overwhelming success of the movement, which, for a time, dominated the face of evangelicalism, caused some to reexamine what being an evangelical meant, including women, ethnic believers, and African-Americans. Was it mainly a platform for white guys waving fists in stadiums?

At the same time, for many evangelicals, political apathy was setting in. The deflating candidacy defeat of Bob Dole in 1996 and cultural/political issues that remained unresolved in their minds—partial-birth abortion, the push for the legalization of gay marriage—moved evangelicals to broaden relationships with other faith communities. New alliances formed between Catholics and evangelicals, and a wider conversation unfolded with Orthodox and mainline denominations, all of which were looking for answers to bewildering social and cultural challenges confronting faith communities.

By the late 1990s the evangelical movement had clearly matured in some ways. Its academic institutions were being taken more seriously. Efforts were being made to reach out to the gay community. Pariahs like Fred Phelps, who waved his hellfire signs at funerals of gay people (and oversaw the website www. godhatesfags.com), were decisively condemned by evangelicals. Renegades who killed abortion doctors and bombed clinics were equally condemned; many evangelicals have made sincere efforts to find new ways to address the abortion debate.

In other ways, however, the "evangelical movement," as it has been known, has also been coming apart. Women and minorities have felt disenfranchised. Intellectuals have felt embarrassed. Activists have felt discouraged. Those on the left have criticized policies of brothers and sisters on the right (and vice versa). Unmarried and divorced evangelicals have felt alienated because of the community emphasis on "family values." (Divorce rates among evangelicals easily equal those of non-evangelicals.) *The Simpsons'* Ned Flanders hasn't offered much comic relief.

NOT YOUR FATHER'S EVANGELIST

Inevitably, the Billy Graham era was reaching its sunset. For the latter half of the twentieth century, evangelicals seemed to rally around that name—a name all Americans could revere. It is not only evangelicals who have wondered who will be "the next Billy Graham."

Expectations have focused on the Graham offspring. Franklin Graham received the public blessing from his father in May 1998 at a crusade in Albuquerque. But it had been already officially conferred a few years before when, in 1995, the board of directors of the Billy Graham Evangelistic Association (BGEA) unanimously elected Franklin as vice chair "with direct succession as chair and chief executive officer should his father ever become incapacitated."

The succession question is a challenge for the evangelical community at this time, because so many of its primary institutions and organizations were launched by visionary personalities like Graham (and Campus Crusade's Bill Bright, who recently passed away). It cuts one way into the heart of institutional concerns about preserving the founder's vision (and keeping the dollars coming in), while posing the vexing question: Is keeping "the institution" alive God's movement, or capitulation to a constituency? How does anyone fill the shoes of a giant?

This dilemma encapsulates the evangelical challenge of the twenty-first century. The time is upon us when old formulas—like the Four Spiritual Laws or the belting baritone of the Graham crusades' George Beverly Shea—no longer work as viable means of reaching people with the Gospel. This has been due in part to forces beyond their control. We live in an age of unprecedented change, connection, and information, which, in turn, have shaped the sensibilities of the upcoming generation that will soon lead evangelicalism.

In a way, the advent of the new millennium has meant, for evangelicalism, a season of reexamination. What *does* it mean to be an evangelical? Who will lead them into the future and give the movement a congenial face the way Billy Graham did over this past half century?

Regardless of political persuasion, many evangelicals remained ambivalent during the 2000 elections and, surprisingly, did not come out in hordes to support the "born-again" candidate George W. Bush. His first campaign did not pull out the stops when it came to reaching out to this constituency. Bush knew evangelicals and understood their language. He held a handful of preelection meetings with them. But that was as far as it went.

As for the 2004 election, social commentators largely agree that religion and morality played a significant role in the outcome. Evangelicals made the difference for George W. Bush, slim though it was. They were energized primarily over abor-

---

Facts and Figures: Goers and Makers

According to pollster George Barna, those who have said yes to the following affirmations are considered evangelicals:

- They believe faith is very important in life.
- They believe they have a responsibility to share their beliefs about Jesus.
- They believe Satan exists.
- They believe eternal salvation is possible only through grace (not works).
- They believe Jesus lived a sinless life on earth.
- They believe God is all-knowing, all-powerful, and perfect, and that he created the universe and continues to sustain it.

In 2004, according to a Barna poll, 14 to 16 million Americans said yes to these affirmations. Twenty-nine percent of them have college degrees (higher than the national average), and 84 percent are registered to vote (6 percent are registered Democrats, 14 percent registered Republicans, and 5 percent independents).

---

tion and the legalization of gay marriage. One poll, at this writing, noted that 86 percent of evangelicals support George W. Bush. In any case, most experts concur that from 2004 on, both sides of the political spectrum will summon no small measure of religious rhetoric in their campaigns, much of it an attempt to reach evangelicals.

One thing is clear: evangelicals do not vote as a bloc. They are, rather, individual citizens with strongly held religious convictions that compel them to act or respond according to personal conscience. Their primary unifying and defining feature in any case, as noted throughout their tumultuous history, has been that they are a band of "goers" and "makers" ("Go therefore and make disciples of all nations" [Matthew 28:19]). They have answered this call on many fronts, and with heightened social consciousness, and their efforts have made an impact beyond their small numbers.

FAITH-BASED SOCIAL PROGRAMS AND THE RESTORATIVE JUSTICE MOVEMENT

After his first election in 2000, when President George W. Bush held his initial meeting in the White House to discuss prospects for faith-based initiatives, Charles Colson attended. The president made a "passionate plea," said Colson, for the viability of faith-based solutions to today's many social problems. One question continually arose: How do we know this will work? The president turned to Colson. "Chuck Colson over here can tell you it works." Bush was referring to the Inner-Change Fellowship Initiative (IFI) program that, as governor of Texas, he had helped Colson initiate in Houston. IFI offers prisoners a daily disciplined routine of private and group devotions, classes in the Bible, communal meals, work, study, and worship. Participants were hardly peach-faced seminarians— they were criminals serving time for child molesting, drug dealing, and murder. Their lexicon included phrases like "twenty-five years with an 85 percent mandatory."

As evidence of the effectiveness of faith-based programs, Colson pointed to the recidivism numbers since the first "graduating" class of the IFI program—under 5 percent, which, in general prison terms, is unheard of. According to Jack Cowley, the national director of operations for IFI, typical recidivism rates among the general prison population hover around 50 percent.

This is an example of the evangelical approach to justice, which is restorative, not retributive. It is aimed at "changing the heart," as candidate George W. Bush said when explaining why Jesus was his favorite philosopher. Restorative justice means the restoration of the victim *and* the criminal through admission of guilt, acts of contrition, pleas for forgiveness, and forgiveness conferred. Dan Kingery, prison counselor and veteran with the Iowa judicial department as a juvenile court officer and in juvenile probation, explained, "There are a lot of good-hearted people that have great intentions. But they don't address the heart of man. That's where the change has to take place. These men and their crimes have destroyed their families, have stolen the future from their children, and have stolen safety from our communities. These men have a huge impact." Restorative justice takes the crime away from the state and connects it more closely with the victimized individual or community, which, said Kingery, can have a positive ripple effect. "The restorative justice movement has opened a door of service to the faith community that has not been opened in the past."

Another point of impact has been in faith-based programs aimed at youth, especially abstinence programs like True Love Waits and Sex Respect. Evangelicals have embraced these programs as an alternative to sex education that focuses on contraception and safe sex. Starting in 1993 True Love Waits, a Baptist initiative, waged a campaign in high schools and on college campuses inviting students to remain abstinent until marriage. They continue to distribute "covenant cards," which young people sign, stating: "Believing that true love waits, I make a commitment to God, myself, my family, my friends, my future mate, and my future children to be sexually abstinent from this day until the day I enter a biblical marriage relationship."

The Sex Respect program, a curriculum used in more than 2,500 schools in the seventh, eighth, ninth, and tenth grades, teaches young teens that saying no to premarital sex is their right, is in the best interest of society, and is in the spirit of true sexual freedom. Creator Coleen Kelly Mast, who is Catholic, created a program that emphasizes "self-control, not birth control."

According to the Centers for Disease Control and Prevention (CDC), between 1991 and 2001 the percentage of U.S. high school students who had sexual intercourse fell from 54.1 percent to 45.6 percent. The percentage of high school students reporting multiple sex partners (defined as four or more) has also declined. Evangelicals do not claim all the credit for these positive trends. But their activism sparked the efforts to address staggering numbers of sexually transmitted diseases and sexual promiscuity among youth.

Not all abstinence programs emphasize the Bible. But evangelicals ignited the efforts of many, including parents and schools, community organizations, health-care organizations, and nonevangelical faith-based organizations. Most notably, they've won the commitment of adolescents themselves, who hold the future of evangelicalism.

THE NEW GENERATION

Today's youth have been the subject of much of the recent cultural conversation. The string of school shootings over the past few years has aroused national soul-searching and has highlighted the extremes, positive and negative, of the generation known as the Millennials, those born in the 1980s and '90s.

One of the most positive viewpoints is found in the recently published *Millennials Rising* (Vintage) by William Strauss and Neil Howe, who assert that the Millennials are a generation "birthmarked for greatness," a do-gooder generation. Strauss and Howe neglect a notable trend, however, that accounts in part for this heroic inclination.

"The unsung story of today's teenagers may be how religious they are," wrote John Leland in an article in *Newsweek*. In the piece, Conrad Cherry, director of the Center for the Study of Religion and American Culture at Indiana University/Purdue, says, "We are witnessing a new revival of religion." According to Barna, 84 percent of this age group say religious faith is very important, and more than 80 percent describe themselves as Christian. At the same time, two out of three teens strongly desire a personal relationship with God, but fewer than half are excited about church.

Trends and demographics are open to interpretation. But two characteristics consistently emerge as defining features of the Millennials: They are activists and they long for God. Many churches grope for ideas about how to reach this complicated and disparate cohort, and the Millennials themselves express ambivalence about the institutionalized church. One place where the evangelical church and Millennials have come together is the mission trip. This experience is becoming so prevalent in Christian youth ministry that many high school pastors see it almost as a rite of passage.

All of this appeals to the activist and spiritual longings so evident in today's youth. "Youth pastors see the opportunity in the lives of today's youth to call them to a higher level of accountability. The youth are answering that call," said Seth Barnes, executive director of Adventures in Missions (www.adventures.org), which sponsors and facilitates trips for youth groups around the country. The exponential rise in the number of trips highlights the point. In 1979, short-term mission trips numbered around 25,000 that year. By 1989 that number had jumped to 120,000, and by 1995 to 250,000. Barnes says the mission trip has moved from being "a fad to a phenomenon."

WOMEN AS MINISTERS

Another major trend in evangelical missions has been the active leadership roles being assumed by women. This highlights an area of contradiction and controversy that has hobbled attempts toward unity in the contemporary evangelical movement. The role of women in leadership roles and as candidates for ordained ministry drew national attention in June 2000 when the Southern Baptist Convention included a statement in its confession of faith that said, "Both men and women are gifted for service in the church, [but] the office of pastor is limited to men as qualified by Scripture," referring to Paul's epistle to Timothy: "A woman should learn in quietness and full submission. I do not permit a woman to teach or to have authority over a man; she must be silent" (1 Timothy 2:11–12). This is an example of the way scripture can be used to advance a particular point of view. Just as many believe that according to Paul, women cannot be ministers, others assert equally that women can indeed be ministers, also based on Paul. For example, he calls Phoebe a minister in Romans 16, and in his letter to the Galatians he says, "There is neither Jew nor Greek, there is neither slave nor free man, there is neither male nor female; for you are all one in Christ Jesus" (Galatians 3:28).

Nevertheless, the Southern Baptists, who made gender an issue of confession in their statement of faith, also commission more women as missionaries—who assume leadership roles— than any other denomination. Missions expert Dana Robert noted that women worldwide are "the growth points of the church." Women compose 80 percent of the members of house churches in China; 70 percent in Latin American Pentecostal churches; and 70 to 80 percent in African churches. The largest church in Seoul, South Korea, has seven hundred pastors, most of them women, plus fifty-two thousand neighborhood cells that are led almost entirely by women.

As a result, evangelical mission boards are making conscious attempts to include women in regional leadership positions and to empower them on the field. Interserve was started by women in the 1960s and has women in regional leadership positions throughout the world. Frontiers has sponsored conferences to promote missions focusing specifically on ministries to Muslim women.

There has been a shift away from the "imperialistic" missions model to one that is more focused on customs of and relationships with the local people.

Relief agencies such as World Relief attract many women to their mode of hands-on service, and the agencies are thrilled to have them. One country served by World Relief is Cambodia, which has the highest death rate among children in East Asia (17 percent of its children do not make it to their fifth birthday) and a majority population of women (64 percent). World Relief brought its microenterprise development ministries (training women to run their own small businesses) to the slums of Phnom Penh. Joke van Opstal, a registered nurse with World Relief, began a puppet ministry to keep children occupied while their mothers were in the program. Through puppet stories, she taught children about the need for better hygiene and at the same time told them about a God who loves them. "We do half health-care stories and half evangelism," she says.

World Relief president Clive Calver (who has since left the organization) says, "Microenterprise development means child survival. Child survival means Kids Clubs. Kids Clubs mean evangelism. Evangelism means church planting."

PUBLISHING BOOST

In the 1980s Phyllis Tickle, contributing religious editor of *Publishers Weekly*, predicted that books would soon become "portable pastors." Her prediction has proven true. Now more than at any other time in recent history, religious and spiritual publishing has surpassed all genres. Lynn Garrett, religious editor of *PW,* credits evangelical publishing for the increase. "With the resurgence of evangelical Christianity in the late '70s and early '80s, religious book publishing attained its highest rate of growth," she says. Bill Anderson, CEO of the Christian Booksellers Association, noted: "Christian retail stores saw a 47 percent increase in sales growth over the past five years." Best-sellers like the Left Behind series and Christian self-help books

---

More Facts and Figures: Who Are the Evangelicals?

- Thirty-seven percent of all Christians describe themselves as born again or evangelical; that includes nearly half of all Protestants (47 percent), as well as a small share (14 percent) of Catholics.

- Baptists still dominate: Sixty-two percent of Baptists say they're evangelical Christians, compared to 46 percent of all other Protestant denominations combined and 37 percent of nondenominational Protestants.

- Evangelism soars particularly among blacks and Southerners: Two-thirds of blacks describe themselves as evangelical or born-again Christians, double the share of whites who do so. And 55 percent of Christians in the South say they're born again, compared to 21 percent in the Northeast, 26 percent in the Midwest, and 31 percent in the West.

- Lower-income Christians also are more apt to be evangelicals. Among those with household incomes under $35,000, 45 percent are evangelicals; among those with higher incomes this figure declines to 31 percent.

Source: ABC News/Beliefnet poll conducted by telephone June 20–24, 2004, among a random national sample of 1,022 adults.

---

like Bruce Wilkinson's *The Prayer of Jabez* and *The Purpose Driven Life* by Rick Warren, pastor of the Saddleback Church in Lake Forest, California, have become publishing phenomena, appealing to Christians of a variety of traditions as well as to the spiritually curious—and exposing huge numbers of readers to the evangelical message.

Evangelical Etiquette

AT CHURCH

> Bring your own Bible.
>
> Be prepared to sing "Shine, Jesus, Shine."
>
> Be ready to fill out the visitor registration form in the pew rack.
>
> Don't be surprised if some folks wave their hands in the air.
>
> Be prepared to shake hands with people in neighboring pews when the pastor directs it.
>
> Be ready to watch the pastor preach or follow the words of the hymn on the TelePrompTer (megachurches only).
>
> Dress: Casual.

AT BIBLE STUDY

> Bring your own Bible.
>
> Be prepared to answer the question "What has God laid on your heart about that passage?"
>
> Be ready to be asked if you have any prayer requests.
>
> Be ready to deal with being asked to pray out loud (but feel no obligation to do so).
>
> Sign up to bring food.
>
> Dress: Casual.

──────────── How Come? ────────────

Billy Graham Trivia Quiz

1. How many people has Graham preached to in person?

   A. 60 million

   B. 140 million

   C. 210 million

   D. 480 million

   [Answer: C]

2. In how many countries has he preached?

   A. 37

   B. 55

   C. 153

   D. 185

   [Answer: D]

3. A crusade in what city brought Graham to public attention?

   A. Los Angeles

   B. London

   C. Mexico City

   D. Atlanta

   [Answer: A]

4. Where did Graham study?

   A. Notre Dame

   B. Rice College

   C. Harvard Divinity School

   D. Wheaton College

   [Answer: D]

5. How long was Graham's 1957 New York crusade?

A. 4 weeks

B. 16 weeks

C. 8 weeks

D. 6 weeks

[Answer: B]

6. Where are the Billy Graham Evangelistic Association headquarters?

A. Minneapolis

B. Houston

C. Detroit

D. Charlotte

[Answer: D]

7. What is the name of Billy Graham's periodical?

A. *His Word*

B. *Decision*

C. *The Way*

D. *Faith*

[Answer: B]

8. What book by Billy Graham published in 1997 was on three Top 10 lists at once?

A. *The Mercy of God*

B. *Evangelism: Spreading His Word*

C. *Just As I Am*

D. *Be Not Afraid*

[Answer: C]

9. Where was Graham born and raised?

A. North Carolina

B. Texas

C. Virginia

D. Minnesota

[Answer: A]

10. What did his father do?

A. Dairy farmer

B. Lawyer

C. Pastor

D. Auto mechanic

[Answer: A]

11. Which of the following books did Graham not write?

A. *Approaching Hoofbeats: The Four Horsemen of the Apocalypse*

B. *How to Be Born Again*

C. *Angels: God's Secret Agents*

D. *Getting Closer to God*

[Answer: D]

12. At what age did Graham decide to become a preacher?

A. 13

B. 16

C. 20

D. 24

[Answer: B]

13. Which of the following statements did Graham not make?

A. Everybody has a little bit of Watergate in him.

B. A real Christian is a person who can give his pet parrot to the town gossip.

C. Comfort and prosperity have never enriched the world as much as adversity has.

D. Your mind cannot possibly understand God. Your heart already knows.

[Answer: D]

14. What did Graham do before becoming an evangelist?

A. Convenience-store clerk

B. Gardener

C. Door-to-door brush salesman

D. Religion teacher

[Answer: C]

15. At what age did Graham preach his first revival?

A. 19

B. 21

C. 26

D. 33

[Answer: A]

16. In what religion was Graham raised?

A. Roman Catholic

B. Baptist

C. Quaker

D. Presbyterian

[Answer: D]

17. What did he study in college?

A. Religion

B. Philosophy

C. Anthropology

D. Finance

[Answer: C]

18. Where was Graham's largest meeting?

A. Seoul (South Korea)

B. Mexico City

C. Chicago

D. Atlanta

[Answer: A]

19. Who of the following gave Graham a Bible with the inscription "To a great teacher in all important matters of humanity and a true friend of Israel?"

A. Golda Meir

B. Moshe Dayan

C. Yitzak Rabin

D. Ariel Sharon

[Answer: A]

20. Who once said Billy Graham, at the pulpit, preached "too loud, too fast" and "pranced around like an uppity pig"?

A) Madalyn Murray O'Hair

B) Barry Lynn

C) Ralph Nader

D) Ruth Bell Graham (his wife)

[Answer: D]

Conclusion:
"Until They Rest in God"

When outsiders get to know evangelicals, they often express shock that they actually like them. That is because evangelicals are not a voting bloc, or an institution, or an arm of Western imperialism, but a thirsty people who, in their view, are trying to lead other people to the river that slakes their thirst. As the psalmist says, it is a river that "brings joy to the city of our God" where "God himself lives" (Psalm 46:4–5).

An evangelical can be someone like Charles Colson a.k.a. prisoner number 23226, President Nixon's "hatchet man," who broke rules that landed him in prison, where God changed his life. An evangelical might be someone like Henrietta Mears, a woman ahead of her time in the early twentieth century, who broke stereotypes and the social boundaries of gender in the church. Yet her visionary resolve and tenacity gave rise to the leaders of modern evangelicalism, like the Navigators' Dawson Trotman and Billy Graham. Or an evangelical might be someone like the late Bill Bright, whose approach to the Gospel was simplistic and formulaic, but utterly effective. Or it could be someone like Dr. Amos Bailey, a physician at an inner-city hospital in Birmingham, Alabama, who pioneered the palliative care movement in the United States, which undertakes to ease the pain of dying patients in a compassionate medical setting.

And there are evangelicals like Wendy Wilson, a good neighbor who takes care of the children of her cancer-stricken friend across the street and volunteers as a hospice attendant.

Evangelicals follow Jesus, who was no respecter of the rules dictated by culture, society, or others' expectations. His own disciples were shocked many times when they found him talking to certain people, such as the Samaritan woman who was living with a man not her husband (John 4) or the prostitute with the alabaster jar who washed the feet of Jesus with her tears (Luke 7). The image of Jesus meeting these women highlights the challenge of evangelicalism in the twenty-first century.

Some who are unfamiliar with evangelicals might think they have too many rules. Yet evangelicals know that a person comes to know God not by following rules but "by grace through faith." How does one determine who is living in sin and who is not? How does one calculate who is closer to the throne of God? Who is in the club, and who's out? What is that line of separation and where is it drawn?

Evangelicals, whoever they are and wherever they live, are still trying to answer that question at a time when it seems there are no rules. The answer they give, insofar as it can be articulated, is this: Follow the Lord Jesus. For time and eternity, he's the one to hang on to. He's the lodestar, "the magnetic north for your compass," as J. I. Packer put it.

Evangelicals come from many callings and vocations. Some are writers; some are activists on the front lines; some are reclusive, pushing people away; some are bullies, pushing people around. Some are adventurers, some academicians. Some preach, some feed the hungry, some buy back slaves, some wave white flags crossing enemy borders. Some of them smoke. Some say curse words. Some have been married and divorced—some more than once. Some watch R-rated movies. Some have children born out of wedlock. Many drink. Do these things diminish them—or anyone—before God?

Evangelicals would have to say no. They, like everyone else, are human. And most tend to be like the man who left the church when the band played "I Can't Get No Satisfaction" at the youth event. He eventually returned. Because, for all their failings, evangelicals seem always to come back to the same place: "No satisfaction"—as Augustine says—"until they rest in God."

antichrist: The prince of the powers of darkness and the enemies of Jesus. He is not Satan himself, but more like Satan's lackey. Paul calls him "the man of lawlessness"; in Revelation he is called "the Beast," who will deceive many prior to the return of Jesus.

baptism: From the Greek word meaning "to immerse." It is a public gesture in which one demonstrably declares identity with Christ, first in burial of the old life (going down into the water), then in resurrection in a new life (coming back up). Evangelicals disagree on the issue of infant baptism. The concept arises from Calvin's theology, in which it is said to be the New Testament version of circumcision.

born again: The phrase used to denote individuals who have been born, not only of flesh and blood through their parents, but also of the Spirit, through a spiritual (inner) awakening that enlivens their identity with Jesus and remolds their inner (and eventually outer) lives.

charismatic: From the Greek word *charisma,* meaning "gift." The term has been appropriated by evangelicals to signify certain worship environments in which the gifts of the Holy Spirit are expressed in exuberant and supernatural manifestations, such as speaking in tongues and healing.

covenant: A contract or agreement between two consenting parties. In the Bible it means the terms outlined by God for living life with his blessing.

doctrine: From the Latin *doctrina*, meaning "teaching" or "teacher." It has taken on additional heft in evangelical circles as a body of principles in a system of belief.

election: Predestination to eternal life, as defined at the Synod of Dort (1616–1619): "The unchangeable purpose of God whereby, before the foundations of the world, out of the whole human race, which fallen by its own fault out of its original integrity into sin and ruin, He has, according to the most free good pleasure of His will, out of mere grace, chosen [to save] in Christ a certain number of specific men, neither better nor more worthy than others." Those chosen for salvation by divine mercy are known as the elect.

enlightenment humanism: The belief that human beings are the standard by which all truth is judged.

final judgment: The moment at the end of time, when all humanity will be judged according to their deeds and confessions while on earth.

glossolalia: From the Greek words *glossa*, (tongue) and *lalia* (chatter); commonly used to refer to the gift of the Holy Spirit of "speaking in tongues" in a heavenly prayer language that is not understood by the person praying, nor by anyone who might hear it.

gospel: Derived from the Anglo-Saxon "God-spell," which means God's story, it refers to the "good news" concerning Christ, the kingdom of God, and salvation. With a capital *G*, it also refers to one of the first four books of the New Testament, which tell of the life, death, and resurrection of Jesus.

holiness movement: Arising in the nineteenth century from the teachings of John Wesley, this movement emphasizes a converted human being's ability to be made holy, that is, free from residual aspects of sin.

intelligent design theory: A sophisticated argument to counter the Darwinian theory of evolution and random natural selection, which is scrutinized for its inexplicable "holes." Intelligent design, or ID, is predicated on the belief that God is the author of life and may have used the evolutionary process to unfold his ongoing creative activity.

justification by faith: The doctrine, arising during the Reformation, that right standing before God is conferred not by the actions or religious duties of a person, but by trust in God's saving activity, realized in the sacrifice of Jesus and manifested by the Holy Spirit.

the Last Supper: The meal Jesus shared with his disciples on the last night of his life. During the meal he instituted what has come to be called "The Lord's Supper": or "communion"; or "the eucharist": eating the bread, which he said "is my body given for you" and drinking the cup which represents "the covenant in my blood."

naturalism: A system of belief declaring that only what can be observed in nature contains the whole of reality.

millennium: From the Latin *milleannus,* meaning a thousand years. In the Bible, it denotes the thousand-year period when Jesus will rule with his church, prior to the final rebellion of Satan (Rev. 20:1–20).

modernism: The movement, arising in the early twentieth century, that attempted to make biblical beliefs compatible with the "modern mind." It diminished the authenticity of biblical narratives that recounted the miraculous.

postmillennialism: The view of the "end times" that understands the millennium to have begun with the birth of the church at Pentecost (when the Holy Spirit descended), and so to have been realized *before* the return of Jesus, as manifest in the ongoing good works and teaching of the church.

predestination: See election.

premillennialism: The "end times" view that asserts the return of Jesus will precede the millennium, at which time he will set up his kingdom and begin his thousand-year reign.

prevenient grace: The prompting of the Holy Spirit to bring about conversion.

saved: See born again.

six-day creationism: The belief in a literal interpretation of Genesis 1, using the "days" of creation as twenty-four-hour time periods. This assigns to the earth a young age and contradicts the fossil record, as it is presently understood. Those who hold to this view are "a dwindling group," according to one expert in this field.

sola scriptura: From the Latin meaning "scripture alone." A teaching, promulgated by Luther during the Reformation, that the Bible (as opposed to rituals and practices of the church) is the sole source of authority for Christians.

theism: Belief in the existence of God as the creative source of man and the world.

theology: The study of God and God's relation to the world.

universal and apostolic church: The belief in an invisible body of believers, throughout all time, who have authentically borne the ministry of Jesus through the Holy Spirit. Those who belong to the "invisible church," as it is sometimes called, will be made known at the time of the Final Judgment.

SUGGESTED READING:
A PARTIAL LISTING

Classics

Augustine, *Confessions*. New York: Penguin, 1961.

Bunyan, John, *The Pilgrim's Progress*. New York: Penguin Classics, 1965 and 1987.

Sheldon, Charles, *In His Steps*. Grand Rapids: Chosen Books, 1984.

Contemporary

Behe, Michael, *Darwin's Black Box: The Biochemical Challenge to Evolution*. New York: Touchstone, 1996.

Bonhoeffer, Dietrich, *The Cost of Discipleship*. New York: Touchstone, 1995.

Colson, Charles, *Born Again*. Grand Rapids: Chosen Books, 2004.

Dobson, James, *The New Dare to Discipline*. Wheaton, IL: Tyndale, 1996.

Elliot, Elizabeth, *Shadow of the Almighty*. New York: Harper Collins, 1979.

Fee, Gordon, and Stuart, Douglas, *How to Read the Bible for All It's Worth*. Grand Rapids: Zondervan, 2003.

Lewis, C. S., *Mere Christianity*. New York: HarperCollins, 2001.

Marty, Martin E., *Martin Luther*. New York: Viking/Penguin, 1994.

Noll, Mark, *The Scandal of the Evangelical Mind*. Grand Rapids: Eerdmans, 1994.

Packer, J. I., *Knowing God*. Downers Grove, IL: InterVarsity Press, 1993.

Schaeffer, Francis, *How Shall We Then Live?* Wheaton, IL: Crossway, 1976.

Stott, John, *Basic Christianity*. Grand Rapids: Eerdmans, 1971.

© Steve Sonheim

WENDY MURRAY ZOBA is an award-winning journalist who has covered evangelical Christianity for two decades. She has served as a regional reporter for *Time* magazine and an associate editor and senior writer for *Christianity Today*, and is currently the editor of *GOD Magazine*. She has written a number of books, including *Day of Reckoning: Columbine and the Search for America's Soul* and *Facing Forward*, a memoir.

PHILIP YANCEY, one of the most beloved Christian authors today, has written books that in total have sold more than 14 million copies, including *The Jesus I Never Knew, Rumors of Another World, Where Is God When It Hurts?, What's So Amazing About Grace?*, and *Soul Survivor*.

BELIEFNET is the leading multifaith spirituality and religion Web site. Through its newsletters and Web site, Beliefnet reaches 4 million people daily. It is the winner of numerous prestigious awards, including the Webby for Best Spirituality Site and the Online News Association's top award for general excellence for independent Web sites. Its book *Taking Back Islam* won the Wilbur Award for Best Religion Book of 2003.